Vanishing Wilderness of
Antarctica

WHITE STAR PUBLISHERS

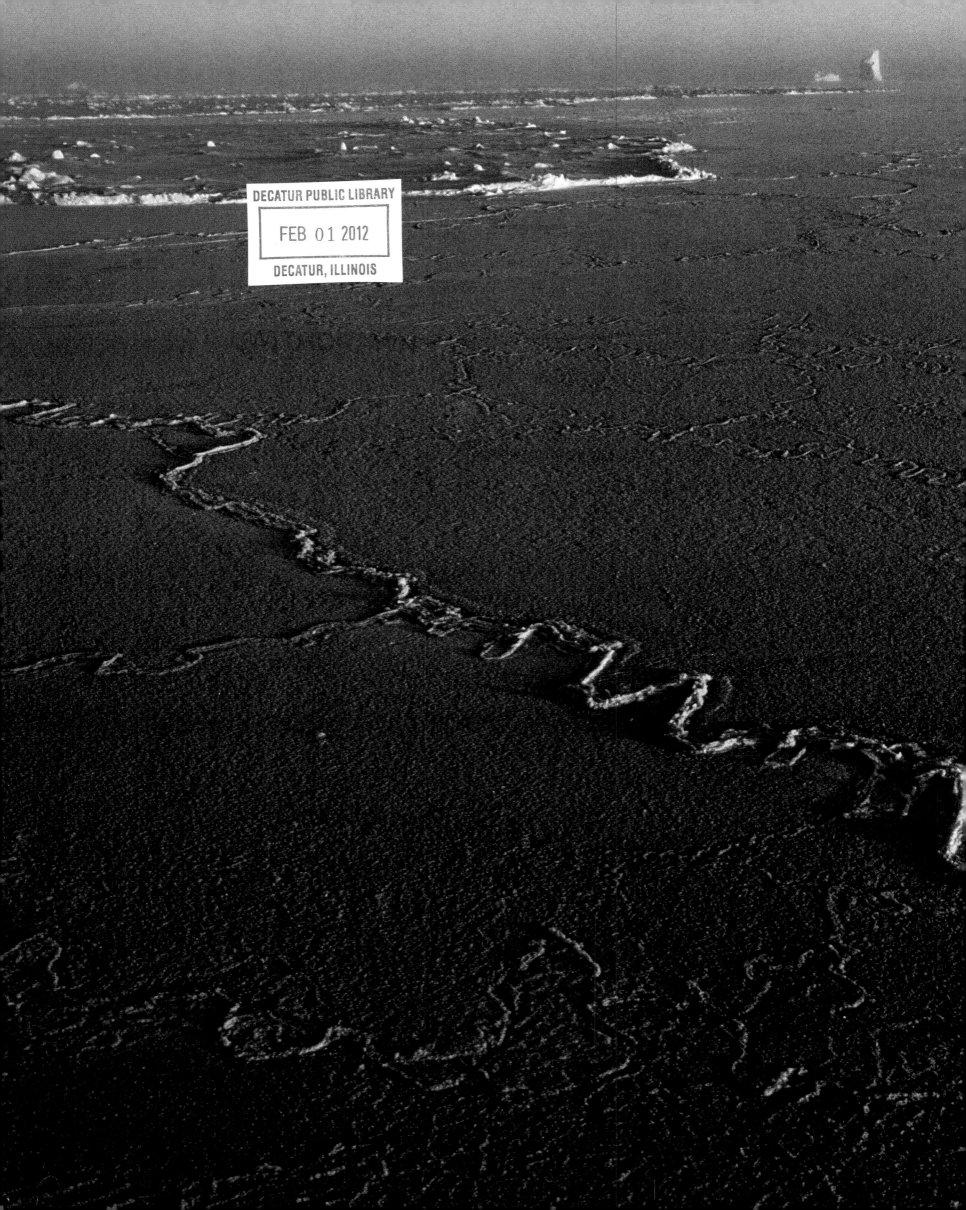

Contents

EDITED BY
VALERIA MANFERTO DE FABIANIS

TEXT
COLIN MONTEATH

GRAPHIC DESIGN
MARIA CUCCHI

1 FROM LEFT: GENTOO PENGUINS (PYGOSCELIS PAPUA) SURFING; A MASSIVE TABULAR ICEBERG; A WEDDELL SEAL (LEPTONYCHOTES WEDDELLII).

2-3 WHEN THE SOUTHERN OCEAN FREEZES OVER DURING WINTER HUGE FLOES OF SEA ICE FORM. THESE FLOES PILE UP TOGETHER TO FORM ICE WALLS.

4-5 ADELIE PENGUINS (PYGOSCELIS ADELIAE) SCRAMBLE OVER THE PACK ICE BENEATH AN OLD, WEATHERED ICEBERG IN THE ROSS SEA.

6-7 THE EMPEROR PENGUIN (APTENODYTES FORSTERI) COLONY ON THE SEA ICE AT ATKA BAY IN THE WEDDELL SEA FRAMED BY A LARGE CAVERN IN AN ICEBERG.

8-9 YOUNG ELEPHANT SEAL (MIROUNGA LEONINA) PUPS LIE TOGETHER ON A SOUTH GEORGIA BEACH, WITH KING PENGUINS (APTENODYTES PATAGONICUS) BEHIND. THESE ELEPHANT SEALS WILL SPEND THE WINTER TOTALLY AT SEA.

10-11 CHINSTRAP PENGUINS (PYGOSCELIS ANTARCTICUS) ON AN OLD BLUE ICEBERG NEAR CANDLEMAS ISLAND, ONE OF THE SOUTH SANDWICH ISLANDS.

13 A SMALL ICEBERG IS PERFECTLY REFLECTED IN THE MIRROR CALM WATERS OF PARADISE BAY, ANTARCTIC PENINSULA.

Foreword

Antarctica

*A*ntarctica is breathtakingly beautiful and the quintessential wild place. It is our planet's ultimate cold desert, a high, windy plateau of ice that supports almost no life. Paradoxically, the coastal regions and the ocean surrounding Antarctica teem with life, and much of it is unique to these high latitudes. No one owns Antarctica and there are no national parks or nature reserves in the conventional sense. The whole of the seventh continent should be thought of as a World Park, to be preserved in perpetuity for all to wonder at and enjoy. It is remarkable that an entire continent can be set aside strictly for peaceful purposes, as a place for scientific research, for the preservation of wildlife, for low-impact recreation, and, inspired by its wilderness values, simply for the spiritual nourishment of all.

The continent is wild and free and thanks to the remarkable vision of the 1959/61 Antarctic Treaty everything beyond 60 degrees South will thankfully remain so. The Antarctic Treaty was originally signed by seven nations, but now it is honored by 46 countries, most of which maintain year-round research stations. The clauses of the treaty include many sensible conservation measures, the prohibition of the dumping of nuclear waste, and it also expressly excludes military activity unless in the support of science.

Antarctica is an isolated, ice-covered landmass and its sheer immensity is hard to grasp. It covers 5.4 million sq miles (14 million sq km) and is almost twice the size of the United States. Although extremely mountainous its highest summit, the Vinson Massif, is only 16,049 ft (4,892 m), which is not high by world standards. However, the vertical relief and grandeur of the peaks in the Ellsworth and Transantarctic ranges are equal to anything in the Himalaya. Surprisingly, there are even active volcanoes in Antarctica. And yet, except for the famous Dry Valleys of South Victoria Land, there is almost no ice-free land anywhere. What little soil there is is poor and thin, but some vegetation does manage to grow and a limited number of specially adapted plant species, such as lichens, survive on rocks, eking out an existence within a few hundred miles of the South Geographic Pole. Some have even adapted to live within the rocks themselves. There are a few mosses and grasses that live on the outer fringes of the continent. This paucity of plant species is in marked contrast to the Arctic, where some 100 species of higher plants flourish.

The Arctic is an ocean surrounded by continents, but Antarctica is a continent surrounded by a mighty ocean, the Southern Ocean, which is the coldest and most tempestuous body of water imaginable. It is also a nutrient-rich ocean that supports an enormous biomass. In winter, the Southern Ocean freezes into a grinding, iron-hard mosaic of sea ice, effectively doubling the size of the continent. The reflective, albedo effect of this much ice is considerable and the combined influence of Antarctica and the Southern Ocean has far-reaching consequences for global weather systems and ocean circulation patterns, even in the northern hemisphere. Giant tabular icebergs that break off the ice shelves are a common feature of Antarctica, with some of them measuring hundreds of miles in length.

Today, there is an acceptance that human impact on the planet, notably by the burning of fossil fuels, has contributed significantly to global warming. This has emphasized the vital importance of both polar regions as sensitive indicators of climate change. The Antarctic Peninsula, that long mountainous finger that points towards South America, is warming up faster than anywhere else on the planet. Dramatically, entire glacier and ice-shelf systems have collapsed in the last decade, which are unprecedented events in recorded glaciological history. The consequences for even more rapid ice loss are profound, with the potentiality of a rise in world ocean levels likely to affect many island communities.

Antarctica and the Southern Ocean support a rich diversity of wildlife, much of it found nowhere else. Although there is not a great diversity of species in Antarctica, compared with the Arctic, they occur in great numbers. The foundation of Antarctica's food chain is the shrimp-like krill and the vast swarms of these tiny crustaceans support huge numbers of seabirds, penguins, and seals. These marine creatures spend a large proportion of their time roaming the Southern Ocean in search of krill and small fish so they can feed their young, which are hatched or born during the short austral summer months from October to January. The filter-feeding baleen whales also depend on krill. Now that the industrial slaughter of Antarctic whales has stopped, more and more cetaceans have been observed feeding in Southern Ocean waters. Even though the Japanese persist in operating a small pelagic Antarctic whaling fleet, the Southern Ocean has now been declared a whale sanctuary — a place where whale populations can recover and hopefully find peace and solace after the merciless killing of the past.

It is for its penguins, of course, that Antarctica is perhaps most famous. Penguins are impressively tough little seabirds with their black and white tuxedo appearance and Chaplinesque waddle. Although flightless, penguins swim underwater as if they were flying, but it is when they are on land during the breeding season that visitors become totally enamored with their appealing antics. Of the 17 species, only the Adelie, gentoo, chinstrap, and emperor breed on or around the continent, with the largest of all penguins, the emperor, laying its egg in the total darkness and mind-numbingly cold depths of winter. The other penguins, such as the king, rockhopper, and yellow-eyed, occupy colonies on the subantarctic islands that encircle the Southern Ocean, largely in the Roaring Forties.

Amid a vast Southern Ocean, the far-flung specks of the subantarctic islands are the jewels in the Antarctic crown. Campbell, Macquarie, Kerguelen, Crozet, and Heard, to name a few, are unique southern hemisphere environments.

The complex plant communities found on these islands as well as the nesting sites for various seabirds, such as petrels, penguins, and albatrosses, make them precious sanctuaries. Today, now that the bloody sealing era is over, the governments of New Zealand, Australia, France, and South Africa jealously protect these fragile islands, and most have now been designated as nature reserves or UNESCO World Heritage Sites. One of the most urgent and vital tasks is to keep foreign plant species out and to eradicate any remaining introduced animal pests, particularly cats and rabbits.

Lying on the wind-battered boundary between the Antarctic and subantarctic, the heavily glaciated island of South Georgia is perhaps the most beautiful island of all. South Georgia has a mountainous landscape with a verdant foreshore of tussock grass. The surf-pounded beaches are crowded with king penguins, elephant seals, and fur seals. Wheeling overhead there is a myriad of other seabirds, notably the majestic wandering and light-mantled sooty albatrosses. All of the subantarctic islands have a complex human history too, involving explorers, sealers, whalers, and, in more recent years, scientists, artists, and mountaineers.

Everything about Antarctica and its subantarctic islands is wild, and yet Antarctica has a softer side as well. There can be utter calm, which brings a welcome though undoubtedly brief respite from the wind, when even the low-angled sun can feel warm. At such times, it is a joy to observe the majestic fjords, with the mountain peaks, glaciers, and icebergs reflected perfectly in the mirrored surface of their waters – utter peace and beauty. The polar regions are especially beautiful during a long, lingering dawn or dusk, when the entire landscape is bathed in delicate pastel colors that illuminate the intricate textures in the snow and rock.

In a world that is overpopulated and where plant and animals species, indeed entire eco-systems, are under threat of extinction, Antarctica remains a beacon of hope that humans can look after an entire continent. It has often been said that if we cannot preserve Antarctica then what can we save? Thankfully, we have recognized Antarctica's irreplaceable wilderness values and cherish them for what they are. Above all, in a noisy, cluttered world, where it is increasingly hard to find peace and calm, Antarctica's greatest blessing is silence.

18-19 GENTOO PENGUINS (PYGOSCELIS PAPUA) WADDLE DOWN THE BEACH PAST AN ELEPHANT SEAL (MIROUNGA LEONINA) AND INTO THE SURF AT GOLD HARBOUR, SOUTH GEORGIA.

20-21 JUVENILE WANDERING ALBATROSSES (DIOMEDEA EXULANS) STRETCH THEIR MASSIVE WINGS IN A COURTSHIP DISPLAY IN THE TUSSOCK GRASS OF ALBATROSS ISLAND, SOUTH GEORGIA.

22-23 CHINSTRAP PENGUINS (PYGOSCELIS ANTARCTICUS) HITCH A RIDE ON A LEDGE BENEATH A GIANT TABULAR ICEBERG ADRIFT IN THE SCOTIA SEA.

24-25 MIST RISING FROM A PEAK ON GOUDIER ISLAND. PEAKS LIKE THESE ARE TYPICAL OF THE MOUNTAINOUS SPINE OF THE ANTARCTIC PENINSULA.

South America

South Georgia

Falkland Islands

South Shetland Island

Deception Islands

Antarctic Peninsula

Pacific Ocean

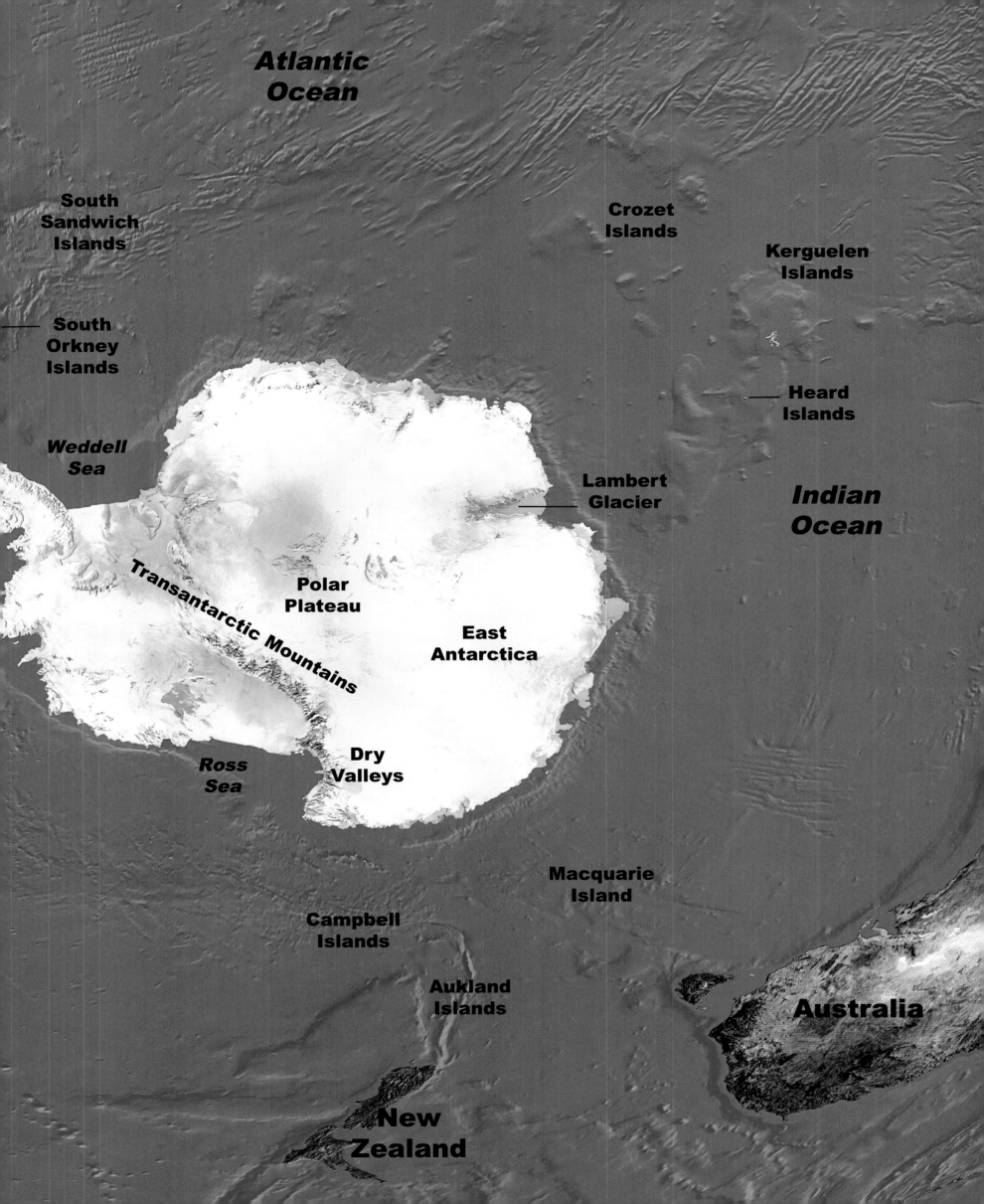

The Polar Plateau

It is hard to comprehend the massive expanse of Antarctica's interior which is divided into two regions – the truly vast and high East Antarctic Ice Sheet and the smaller, lower West Antarctic Ice Sheet. Together they form what is known as the Polar Plateau, a desert of ice 5.4 million sq miles (14 million sq kms) in area that is centred around the South Geographic Pole at 90 degrees South (this is not to be confused with the South Magnetic Pole or the South Geomagnetic Pole – see below). It is vitally important to understand the mechanisms and rates of present-day climate change, and the ice cores recovered from several drilling projects throughout the Polar Plateau not only reveal a detailed record of the world's past climates and other natural events, such as volcanic eruptions, but also human activity, including nuclear explosions in the northern hemisphere and airborne pollutants. The Polar Plateau is one of the world's harshest environments and it is perhaps the last true wilderness as there is almost no permanent human presence.

The Polar Plateau has an average depth of 7,500 ft (2,300 m), though depths of up to 16,400 ft (5,000 m) have been recorded. It is an ice desert, where the water equivalent of only 1 inch (2 cm) of dry, powder snow falls annually, and locks up 75 percent of the world's fresh water. As there is virtually no melt, what little snow that does fall simply gets blown around and accumulates. The snow layers are gradually transformed into ice and as the pressure builds at depth the ice behaves almost like molten plastic, flowing under gravity towards the coast. Where the Polar Plateau reaches the East Antarctic coast unimpeded, it forms glaciers such as the mighty Lambert, the largest glacier in the world.

The Lambert is so extensive, powerful, and fast-flowing that where it meets the sea it has formed the floating Amery Ice Shelf, which is a major birthplace for icebergs. In the opposite direction, the barrier formed by the Transantarctic Mountains that dissect the continent blocks much of the flow of ice, daming it up behind the 13,000-ft (4,000-m) high mountains. Where the ice does

break through, glaciers flow seaward, coalescing to form the gigantic Ross Ice Shelf.

The Geographic South Pole is at 9,300 ft (2,835 m) above sea level, hence Antarctica being known as the continent with the highest average elevation on Earth. However, this is not the highest part of the Polar Plateau, as there are a number of massive ice domes, including one near the center of East Antarctica (about 80 degrees South), that reach an elevation of over 13,000 ft (4,000 m). Although the West Antarctic Ice Sheet is much lower it still has elevations of 6,500 ft (2,000 m) above sea level. In places, where the ice flows inland off these high domes, ice streams form, each with its own peculiar (and now much studied) flow patterns.

The Polar Plateau is a windswept desert, a bitterly cold environment that is relentlessly harsh and severely tests any human endeavor. Humans are often pushed close to the limit of what it is possible to endure. There is effectively no animal life here, with only the occasional skua gull observed flying overhead. What little snow falls on the Polar Plateau is dry (there is almost no humidity) and fine, rather like talcum powder. It does not melt and is simply blown about until it drifts into ridges of very compact snow called sastrugi. The waves of sastrugi are often as hard as concrete and they can easily break skis on planes or the heavy caterpillar tracks on an oversnow tractor. Repairing machinery or maintaining buildings in the low temperatures that are the norm on the Polar Plateau can be a desperately difficult, humbling, and potentially life-threatening experience.

The average summer temperature at the U.S. Amundsen-Scott South Pole Station is a nippy -6°F (-21°C), while in winter it drops to a mind-numbingly cold -77°F (-61°C). As the South Geographic Pole is located in the middle of a high continent where it receives little warmth from a low-angled sun, the temperatures are much lower than at the North Pole, which is at sea level and where the Arctic Ocean acts as a heat reservoir. There is continuous sunlight during the austral summer months, but the sun is totally absent from late March until late September.

26-27 THE ELLSWORTH MOUNTAINS CONTAIN THE HIGHEST PEAKS IN ANTARCTICA AND THEY RISE FROM THE POLAR PLATEAU AT 80 DEGREES SOUTH BETWEEN THE BASE OF THE ANTARCTIC PENINSULA AND THE GEOGRAPHIC SOUTH POLE.

27 TOP THE POLAR PLATEAU IS A VAST ICE SHEET WHICH IN PLACES IS UP TO 16,600 FT (5,000 M) THICK. IN CERTAIN LOCATIONS, SUCH AS HERE IN DRONNING MAUD LAND, ROCK PEAKS CALLED NUNATAKS STICK THROUGH THE SURFACE OF THE ICE.

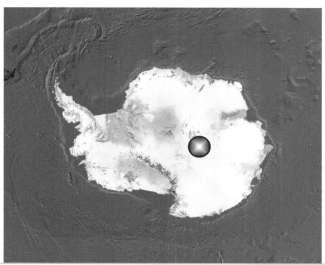

The Polar Plateau

And yet the South Geographic Pole is not the coldest place in Antarctica. That dubious distinction is reserved for the Russian Vostok Station at an altitude of 11,440 ft (3,488 m) in East Antarctica, where the record low is a crippling -128°F (-89°C). During the month of July 1987, the temperature never rose above -97°F (-72°C). Vostok Station is a fascinating place close to the Pole of Inaccessibility (the place that is furthest from the coast). At Vostok, Russian, and now American and French, researchers have built up a solid record of worthwhile science since the station was first built by the Soviets in 1956 during the third International Geophysical Year. Vostok is also close to the South Geomagnetic Pole, which is the place in the southern hemisphere where the Earth's magnetic field, comparable to a tilted dipole bar magnet, intersects with the surface. This makes Vostok one of the best places to study changes in this field. Due to constant shifts in the magnetic field and the fact that the Earth is not a perfect dipole magnet, the South Geomagnetic Pole does not coincide with its "wandering" cousin the South Magnetic Pole, which is currently located beyond the Antarctic Circle in the sea off the coast of Terre Adelie Land.

Vostok sits on 12,100 ft (3,700 m) of ice that is under such pressure that thousands of feet below the surface, near bedrock, a liquid, freshwater lake exists. Discovered in 1996, Lake Vostok is probably the largest of Antarctica's subglacial lakes of which it is thought that there are about 70 in total scattered underneath East Antarctica. Despite the temptation to drill through the ice and examine the 5,400 sq miles (14,000 sq km) of pristine lake water in an attempt to discover what could possibly be unknown organisms, there is much debate about the resulting contamination. Thus far, the Russians have been persuaded to stop drilling just 430 ft (130 m) before penetrating the lake surface. Even so, by studying oxygen and other gas isotopes in the ice core recovered from beneath Vostok, drilling has enabled researchers to look back 420,000 years through four glacial periods.

The Polar Plateau has also been found to be a repository for meteorites that routinely shower Antarctica from outer space. Meteorites fall evenly over the Earth's surface and most fall into the oceans, are buried in soil, or are lost among other rocks. In Antarctica, however, the ones that fall on the Polar Plateau are gradually covered in snow and become embedded in a layer of ice. As the ice moves, the meteorites are transported along with it.

Where the ice dams up behind mountain ranges, the meteorites gradually reappear on the surface as the ice around them ablates. Over the last 30 years, thousands of meteorites have been found concentrated together, scattered on the icy surface at various locations on the edges of the Polar Plateau.

Due to its high elevation with clear, relatively stable air and long dark winters, the Polar Plateau has proved to be an exciting place for astronomy and other upper atmosphere physical sciences, including those associated with the eye-catching displays of Aurora Australis.

The United States has just rebuilt the Amundsen-Scott South Pole Station for a third time so that it can continue its research. Costly though it is to live and work at 90 degrees South, it remains much cheaper than doing the equivalent work from a spacecraft. Other inland stations, such as the Italian/French Concordia Station located at 75 degrees South near Dome C in East Antarctica (opened for year-round operation in 2005), are also making exciting progress with their upper atmospheric research projects. 2007–08 was the fourth International Polar Year with research carried out in both polar regions (the other years were 1882–83, 1932–33, and 1957–58).

During the 21st century, the Polar Plateau will remain one of the most challenging yet precious laboratories that will allow us look through a window into the past and, hopefully, it will also help teach us how to better manage the planet in the future. When seen from space, the Polar Plateau lights up like a magical glowing lantern. Earth the fabled water planet is also an ice planet.

28-29 THE POLAR PLATEAU IS A HIGH WIND-BLOWN DESERT OF VERY DRY SNOW AND ICE. ON AVERAGE ONLY AN INCH (2 CM) OF SNOW FALLS EACH YEAR AND THIS SNOW IS BLOWN BY STRONG WINDS TO FORM VERY HARD RIDGES CALLED SASTRUGI.

30-31 DURING THE DARK WINTER MONTHS FROM MAY UNTIL OCTOBER IT IS COMMON TO WITNESS THE AURORA AUSTRALIS, OR SOUTHERN LIGHTS, A SPECTACULAR, SHIFTING LIGHT SHOW OF IONIZED GASES. THE NEWLY BUILT U.S. AMUNDSEN–SCOTT SCIENTIFIC BASE IS LOCATED AT THE GEOGRAPHIC SOUTH POLE AT AN ALTITUDE OF 9,300 FT (2,835 M).

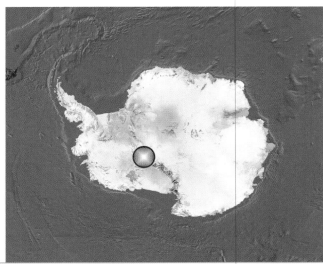

32 TOP THE SHARP-POINTED SUMMITS AROUND THE CALLEY GLACIER REGION ARE TYPICAL OF THE TRANSANTARCTIC MOUNTAINS. SOME PEAKS, SUCH AS THOSE IN THE ROYAL SOCIETY RANGE IN SOUTH VICTORIA LAND, RISE TO OVER 13,000 FT (4,000 M).

32-33 AN AERIAL VIEW OF THE HEAVILY CREVASSED CAMPBELL GLACIER IN THE PRINCE ALBERT MOUNTAINS. THE CAMPBELL IS JUST A MEDIUM SIZE GLACIER BY THE STANDARDS OF THE TRANSANTARCTIC MOUNTAINS.

The Transantarctic Mountains

One of the most dominant features of the entire Antarctic continent is the Transantarctic Mountains that stretch southward for 1,800 miles (3,000 km) from the tip of North Victoria Land on the Ross Sea coast. The jagged sandstone, dolerite, and granite peaks extend in an unbroken chain to reach to within 370 miles (600 km) of the Geographic South Pole, with the icecap of the Polar Plateau rising to meet the mountains at this point. Effectively, the Transantarctic range emerges on the Weddell Sea side of the continent as the Ellsworth Mountains, which contain the loftiest peaks in Antarctica (Vinson Massif at 16,066 ft/4,897 m is the highest), close to the beginning of the mountains of the Antarctic Peninsula. The Transantarctic Mountains divide Antarctica into the massive East Antarctic Ice Sheet and the smaller West Antarctic Ice Sheet, which abuts onto the Antarctic Peninsula.

Although the Transantarctic Mountains are not high by Himalayan or even Andean standards, they do reach 13,000 ft (4,000 m) in places along the Ross Sea coast and so are as beautiful and grand as any peaks on Earth. The fact that they rise from a brutal, storm-tossed, and iceberg-studded sea makes the vertical relief of peaks such as Minto and Herschel seem all the more alluring and impressive. To be caught in wind on these mountains is truly humbling. The low temperatures experienced on the summits are, at best, crippling with temperatures of -40°F (-40°C) quite common. Crucially, the sheer scale of the glaciation engulfing these mountains involves great risks for all who venture there. The overall remoteness and wildness that protects these mountains imparts a unique quality, unrivalled anywhere else.

Further south, glistening in the midnight sun opposite Ross Island, looms the impressive bastion of the Royal Society Range. Almost in the shadow of the Royal Society Range is the moonscape terrain of the Dry Valleys, perhaps the most bizarre environment in Antarctica. The highest summit in the Royal Society Range is Mount Lister at 13,162 ft (4,012 m). Other slightly lower and rarely visited peaks include Huggins, Salient, Hooker, and Rucker spread out along the range. Nearby, lie two ancient, dormant volcanoes Mt. Morning (2,723 m) and Mt. Discovery (2,680 m). These three million-year-old volcanoes stand as guardians to the Ross Ice Shelf, which stretches to the southermost horizon in a gigantic plain of flat, floating ice up to 1,900 ft (600 m) thick. The shelf is formed by glacial ice streams that have coalesced after flowing seawards from the Polar Plateau through the Transantarctic Mountains. Across McMurdo Sound, back on Ross Island lies the active one million-year-old volcano Mt. Erebus 12,450 ft (3,795 m). It makes for a complex and fascinating geological history to have relatively young volcanic rocks lying alongside the ancient rocks of the Transantarctic Mountains. The highest peaks in the southern Transantarctic Mountains are Mt. Miller (13,648 ft/4,160 m), Mt. Markham (14,271 ft/4,350 m), and Mt. Kirkpatrick (14,856 ft /4,528 m). Although they have been climbed, even geologists from the New Zealand and U.S. Antarctic scientific teams rarely visit these peaks. Fossil shells, tree stumps, *Glossopteris* leaves and pollen are all found in the horizontally stratified sandstone beds throughout the Transantarctic Mountains, which is evidence of the earlier epochs when the supercontinent of Gondwanaland experienced a warmer climate.

The most well-known glacier to flow through the Transantarctic Mountains is the Beardmore. First discovered by Ernest Shackleton's British Antarctic expedition of 1908–09, the glacier proved to be a logical access route to the Polar Plateau and a gateway to the South Pole itself. Captain Scott's ill-fated 1911–12 expedition also used this route, which is all the more remarkable as they tried to take ponies pulling laden sledges up its crevassed and icy slopes. Other big glaciers, such as the Darwin, Skelton, Shackleton, Byrd, Nimrod, and Axel Heiberg (Roald Amundsen's route to the South Pole in 1911), all channel enormous quantities of ice down onto the Ross Ice Shelf.

34-35 CLIMBERS ON THE SUMMIT RIDGE OF A TYPICAL ICE-CLAD PEAK IN THE TRANSANTARCTIC MOUNTAINS. SINCE THE EARLY 1960S NEW ZEALAND AND U.S. FIELD RESEARCH PARTIES HAVE CLIMBED MANY PEAKS IN THESE MOUNTAINS, OFTEN AS AN ESSENTIAL PART OF THEIR SCIENTIFIC WORK.

36 THE TRANSANTARCTIC MOUNTAIN PEAKS BEHIND TERRA NOVA BAY RISE FROM SEA LEVEL TO OVER 9,800 FT (3,000 M). LARGE GLACIERS FLOW INTO THE ROSS SEA FROM THE POLAR PLATEAU BEHIND THE MOUNTAINS. TERRA NOVA BAY IS WHERE THE ITALIAN ANTARCTIC RESEARCH PROGRAM HAS ITS SUMMER STATION.

37 MT. KYFFIN IS A DRAMATIC ROCK SPIRE NEAR THE BEGINNING OF THE BEARDMORE GLACIER IN THE HEART OF THE TRANSANTARCTIC MOUNTAINS.

38-39 MIDNIGHT SUN LIGHTS UP THE SUMMIT RIDGES OF MT. HERSCHEL IN THE ADMIRALTY MOUNTAINS IN NORTHEASTERN VICTORIA LAND.

40-41 A LONE FIGURE IS DWARFED BY A GLACIER IN THE ASGARD RANGE IN THE FAMOUS DRY VALLEYS. THE DRY VALLEYS ARE IN THE HEART OF THE TRANSANTARCTIC MOUNTAINS IN SOUTH VICTORIA LAND.

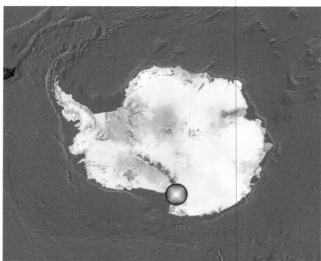

42 TOP AN AERIAL VIEW OF FINGER MOUNTAIN, TAYLOR DRY VALLEY. DARK LAYERS OF DOLERITE ARE SANDWICHED BETWEEN THE CREAMY YELLOW BEACON SANDSTONE.

42-43 THIS AERIAL VIEW OF THE LOWER TAYLOR DRY VALLEY, CLOSE TO MCMURDO SOUND IN THE ROSS SEA, SHOWS THE COMMONWEALTH GLACIER CREEPING DOWN INTO THE SNOW-COVERED VALLEY FLOOR. THE DRY VALLEYS ARE NOT NORMALLY SNOW-COVERED AND THIS FRESH SNOWFALL WILL DISAPPEAR INTO THE DRY ATMOSPHERE VERY QUICKLY. THE ICE-COVERED LAKE FRYXELL CAN BE SEEN TO THE LEFT OF THE GLACIER.

The Dry Valleys

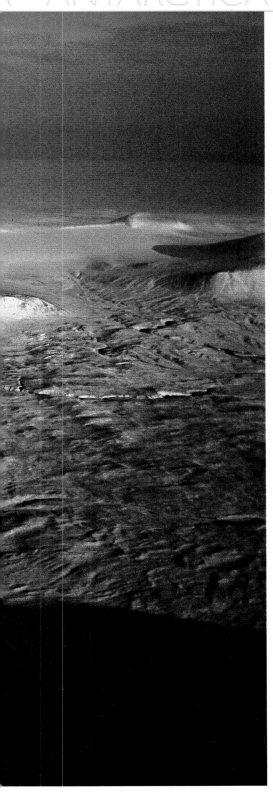

Tucked away in the heart of the Transantarctic Mountains are the Dry Valleys of Southern Victoria Land, one of the most remarkable and beautiful environments anywhere in Antarctica. Ninety-eight percent of the continent is covered by a thick layer of ice, and the remaining two percent consists mainly of these famous valleys situated close to the Ross Sea coast, as well as the less well-known regions of the Bunger, Larseman, and Vestfold hills in East Antarctica. The valley systems are often described as "oases" because they have been virtually ice free for the past 14 million years and so are visually completely different from the vast desert of ice surrounding them. As the glare from the Antarctic ice can be harsh and unforgiving, the Dry Valleys provide a welcome relief for all the senses. There is also a stark contrast between the remnant snub-nosed glaciers and the honeycombed rock peaks, the sweeping scree slopes, and the polygonal mosaics of patterned soil caused by frost heave. For a few brief weeks in midsummer there is even a river. Many visitors are profoundly affected by the quality of the light in the Dry Valleys that, somehow, imparts a sense of peace and tranquility.

The Dry Valleys receive less than 4 inches (100 mm) of snow each year, but as the air is so dry almost all of this precipitation turns into water vapor and is drawn straight back into the atmosphere. The valleys take on a parched, moon-like appearance, and what few bacteria, lichens, and algae that can survive here are not immediately visible, existing only in hidden, niche environments. The slow-moving dry-based glaciers that creep down the hillsides of the Dry Valleys look as if they are truly frozen in time. What little ice that does melt from their glacial snouts in summer helps to feed a number of lakes that remain ice-covered for much of the year.

The Dry Valleys have been formed by the uplift of the Transantarctic Mountains, which act as a dam-like barrier to hold back the ice from the 8,200-ft (2,500-m) high Polar Plateau behind them. Density-driven, katabatic winds funnel down from the Plateau into the valleys, scouring everything in their path, completely desiccating the landscape and re-

lentlessly eroding rocks into fantastic shapes known as ventifacts. Although the wind can be bitterly cold and seemingly relentless, there is some respite with periods of utter calm. While temperatures can climb to a balmy 50°F (10°C) in midsummer, during the long dark winter, from April through to September, they can plummet to a piercingly cold -58°F (-50°C).

Found by Captain Scott's sledging team in 1903, the Dry Valleys captivated the early explorers not only as a place of great beauty but because they enabled their geologists to gain easy access to exposed rock strata. More detailed science in the valleys was undertaken in the late 1950s during the International Geophysical Year and has continued unabated ever since, in part due to the proximity of the New Zealand and U.S. bases on Ross Island, some 50 miles (80 km) away across McMurdo Sound. Geologists have now made detailed studies of the uplift of the sandstone and dolerite formations, analysed the low-grade coal deposits and made collections of fossils, notably from the fossilized tree forest on Mt. Fleming. Biologists, too, have been fascinated by the endolithic lichens that eke out an existence inside the first crystalline layer beneath some rock surfaces. They have also worked on the blue-green algae that survive in thick mats on the lake bottoms. And, remarkably, chemists have discovered "antarcticite," a unique calcium salt crystal that prevents small ponds, such as Don Juan, from freezing.

The Dry Valleys comprise three principal valley systems, the east-west oriented Taylor, Wright, and Victoria valleys, which run parallel to each other and are divided by the turreted peaks of the Asgard and Olympus ranges. The Taylor Valley (named for Griffith Taylor one of Scott's geologists) contains the most extensive glacier in the valleys. At the western extremity of the Taylor, where the Polar Plateau ice has broken through the mountains, the glacier flows relentlessly down the valley. With a backdrop of stunning peaks, the serene and much-studied Lake Bonney lies at the snout of the Taylor, while the smaller Fryxell and Hore lakes lie closer to the sea where the bare rocky valley opens out.

The Dry Valleys

Next door, in the Wright Valley (named for another of Scott's geologists, Charles Wright) a mighty river of ice known as the Airdevronsix icefall tumbles into the head of the valley and flows a short distance before ending abruptly at the entrance to the Labyrinth, which is a complex maze of mini canyons of wind-scoured red rock. At the end of the Labyrinth the Wright Valley splays out again, ending with the tiny glistening jewel of Don Juan Pond that lies just above the extensive and enigmatic Lake Vanda.

Lake Vanda's icy surface presents a delicate network of lace-like cracks that disappear inside the ten-feet thick turquoise ice. This ice covering acts like a giant magnifying glass that captures and concentrates the solar radiation. The trapped energy warms the still, stratified 230-ft (70-m) deep water from zero degrees at the surface to 77°F (25°C) on the lake floor. Only in midsummer does a narrow moat of open water form around Lake Vanda. Mysteriously, the ephemeral, meltwater Onyx River flows inland some 18 miles (30 km) up Wright Valley to empty into Lake Vanda. An eerie sight greets visitors, the bodies of a number of dead Weddell and crabeater seals dotted about Lake Vanda, the lower Wright and other nearby valleys. Somehow they must have become disoriented and strayed inland from McMurdo Sound. After death, in many cases hundreds of years ago, their bodies were preserved by the climate, gradually becoming so desiccated that they are completely mummified.

To the north of Wright Valley lies the exquisite Victoria Valley, which is perhaps the most picturesque of all the Dry Valleys. The Victoria is rarely visited even by government scientists, in part due to the strict level of environmental protection enforced through the Antarctic Treaty's system of SSSI's (Sites of Special Scientific Interest) and SPA's (Specially Protected Areas). Operating under tightly regulated permits, field parties must minimize their impact by removing as much evidence of their work and habitation as possible, including all human waste. No wheeled vehicles are allowed anywhere in the Dry Valleys and access to specific sites is only by helicopter. Described as snug, solar-powered, and spartan, though known for the warmth of its hospitality, New Zealand once occupied Vanda Station, a small summer-only base on the lake's foreshore (three Kiwi teams in the 1960s and 1970s spent the entire winter at Vanda). However, when lake levels rose in the 1980s, the buildings were removed in accordance with the environmental policy.

Although the island of South Georgia is considered the jewel in the Antarctic crown due to the abundance of its wildlife and the wildness of its mountains, the Dry Valleys of Victoria Land are no less special. The extreme nature of the Dry Valleys means they are as close to an alien environment on Earth as could ever be found. Above all, their staggering pristine beauty must be totally respected by all who venture there. The sheer enormity and shifting nature of Antarctic's ice elsewhere means that people's mistakes or overall impact will, to some extent, be covered up, but in the Dry Valleys there is no second chance.

44-45 ICE 10 FT (3 M) THICK COVERS LAKE VANDA IN THE WRIGHT DRY VALLEY.

45 TOP LEFT A LIGHT DUSTING OF SNOW HIGHLIGHTS THE FLOW LINES OF A ROCK GLACIER IN THE BEACON DRY VALLEY.

45 TOP RIGHT AN AERIAL VIEW OF A ROCK GLACIER IN THE BEACON DRY VALLEY, TRANSANTARCTIC MOUNTAINS.

46-47 FLYING ACROSS THE DRY VALLEYS IN SOUTH VICTORIA LAND IS A SPECTACULAR EXPERIENCE. THIS VIEW IS OF THE BEACON VALLEY, WHICH LIES CLOSE TO THE FAMOUS TAYLOR DRY VALLEY. A FRESH SNOWFALL HELPS TO ACCENTUATE THE DARK DOLERITE ROCK AND THE LIGHTER COLORED BEACON SANDSTONE.

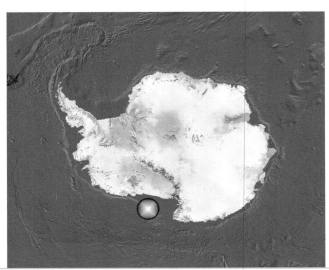

48 TOP A LONE PENGUIN HAS
CLAWED ITS WAY UP ONTO
AN ERODED ICEBERG.

48-49 A SMALL GLACIER FLOWS DOWN
TOWARDS THE COAST OF SOUTH
VICTORIA LAND.

50-51 A LARGE TABULAR ICEBERG FROM
THE ROSS ICE SHELF HAS NOW BROKEN
UP INTO SEVERAL SMALLER ICEBERGS
THAT WILL GRADUALLY DRIFT
NORTHWARDS IN THE ROSS SEA.

ANTARCTICA - ANTARCTICA - ANTARCTICA - ANTARCTIC

The Ross Sea Region

To sail due south from New Zealand, past that country's magnificent subantarctic islands, and into the Ross Sea is to venture into the true heart of Antarctica. For sheer raw beauty, the Ross Sea is surely one of the most incredibly stunning places anywhere in the polar regions. And yet, while the sea can be utterly calm and midsummer temperatures balmy, it has the potential to be perhaps the most ferocious piece of water in the Southern Ocean. The chances of encountering mountainous seas, heavy pack ice, fierce blizzards, and low temperatures are high, requiring total concentration and respect from all mariners. For the early sealers, heading into the jumbled jigsaw of ice floes that stretched across the northern limits of the Ross Sea was almost unthinkable, especially as their vessels had no engines.

Setting out from Hobart in 1842 in two sailing ships, Englishman James Clark Ross defied the predictions of the sealers and succeeded to find a way through the defences of the pack ice and entered the sea that now bears his name. Ross had already been to the Arctic's North Magnetic Pole and was determined to make identical magnetic observations at the opposite end of the Earth, in Antarctica. In this he was frustrated as his instruments told him that the South Magnetic Pole lay beyond an icebound coast dominated by formidable peaks (the Transantarctic Mountains). If Ross were at sea today, he could sail directly over the South Magnetic Pole, because the "wandering pole" has moved significantly over the intervening 170 years and is now located off the coast of East Antarctica, close to the French science station of Dumont d'Urville.

Ross sailed on southward parallel to the Transantarctic Mountains until, at almost 78 degrees South, he made the astounding discovery that two volcanoes blocked his path. He named them Erebus and Terror after his ships and the island on which they were located became known as Ross Island (New Zealand's Scott Base and the U.S. McMurdo Station are situated on Ross Island). That Erebus was obviously an active volcano was a geological

discovery of immense importance. Ross turned eastward to find that Ross Island butted onto an immense flat-topped plain of ice that stretched away to the horizon – the Ross Ice Shelf. This was an impenetrable barrier preventing passage south. Clearly, Ross's discoveries helped to delineate an outline map of Antarctica and significantly paved the way for exploration on land during the so-called "Heroic Era" some 60 years later. It is from bases on Ross Island in the early 1900s that Captain Scott and Ernest Shackleton launched their attempts to reach the Geographic South Pole.

The first sight of land in the northern extremity of the Ross Sea is at Cape Adare in North Victoria Land, which is a wind-ravaged plinth of land that is routinely pounded by heavy surf and churning ice blocks. It was at Ridley Beach, Cape Adare, in 1898, that the British Antarctic Expedition led by the Norwegian Carstens Borchgrevink established a winter base – the first overwinter base on the continent itself. Cape Adare is home to a breeding colony of some 100,000 pairs of Adelie penguins. Their nesting sites are dotted on the bare rocky ground way up onto the headland above Roberston Bay.

Stretching southward as far as the eye can see from Cape Adare are the Transantarctic Mountains, a breath-taking 1,800-mile (3,000-km) long range that swings past the South Geographic Pole to peter out on the Polar Plateau close to the Weddell Sea and the Antarctic Peninsula on the opposite side of the continent. Immense glaciers dissect the Transantarctics to plunge into the Ross Sea or, further south, spread out and form the Ross Ice Shelf.

The 13,658-ft (4,163-m) summit of Mt. Minto dominates the Admiralty Range in the northern part of the Transantarctic Mountains. Closeby, is the lower though more elegant Mt. Herschel, with its sharp-pointed summit of iron-hard ice. Moubray Bay and Cape Hallett beneath Mt. Herschel are home to another large Adelie penguin colony. The cape was once the site for a combined U.S.–New Zealand base that was eventually damaged by fire and abandoned. Here, too, grow luxurious though fragile moss beds. It is now a Specially Protected Area.

The Ross Sea Region

Coulman Island (100 nautical miles south of Cape Hallett), Cape Washington (beneath the active volcano Mt. Melbourne – midway down the Ross Sea coast), and Cape Crozier (at the eastern end of Ross Island) are the principal breeding colonies of emperor penguins in the Ross Sea region. The unique life cycle of the emperor is now well documented and is a remarkable saga of endurance and commitment for the male emperor who incubates the egg on his feet during the darkest winter months.

Emperors build no nest, but simply lay their egg on the ice. In an effective display of teamwork several hundred emperors huddle together to form a windbreak, creating a degree of warmth and protection for the eggs and hatching chicks. Meanwhile the females are at sea hunting fish and krill. As spring approaches she returns to the colony to take over the role of parenting and feeding from the now emaciated father. The breeding success of emperor penguins is always marginal at best, as winter blizzards can sweep across the sea ice to devastate almost an entire generation of chicks. The trumpeting of the emperor penguin is one of the most distinctive and haunting sounds in Antarctica.

52-53 ADELIE PENGUINS (PYGOSCELIS ADELIAE) DIVE INTO THE ROSS SEA FROM AN ICEBERG.

53 ADELIE PENGUINS CAN SWIM UNDER THE WATER EXTREMELY FAST, HOWEVER, THEY MUST LEAP OUT OF THE WATER PERIODICALLY TO BREATH.

The Ross Sea Region

54 A SINGLE EMPEROR PENGUIN (APTENODYTES FORSTERI) CHICK IS HATCHED IN WINTER ON THE SEA ICE AND IS KEPT WARM AND FED BY THE MALE UNTIL THE FEMALE RETURNS FROM THE ROSS SEA WITH MORE FOOD.

55 THERE ARE SEVERAL EMPEROR PENGUINS COLONIES ON THE ROSS SEA COAST AT CAPE ROGET ON COULMAN ISLAND, BENEATH MT. MELBOURNE, AND AT CAPE CROZIER.

56-57 A RAPIDLY GROWING EMPEROR CHICK STANDS BESIDE THE PARENT BIRD IN THE HOPE OF BEING FED MORE SQUID AND KRILL.

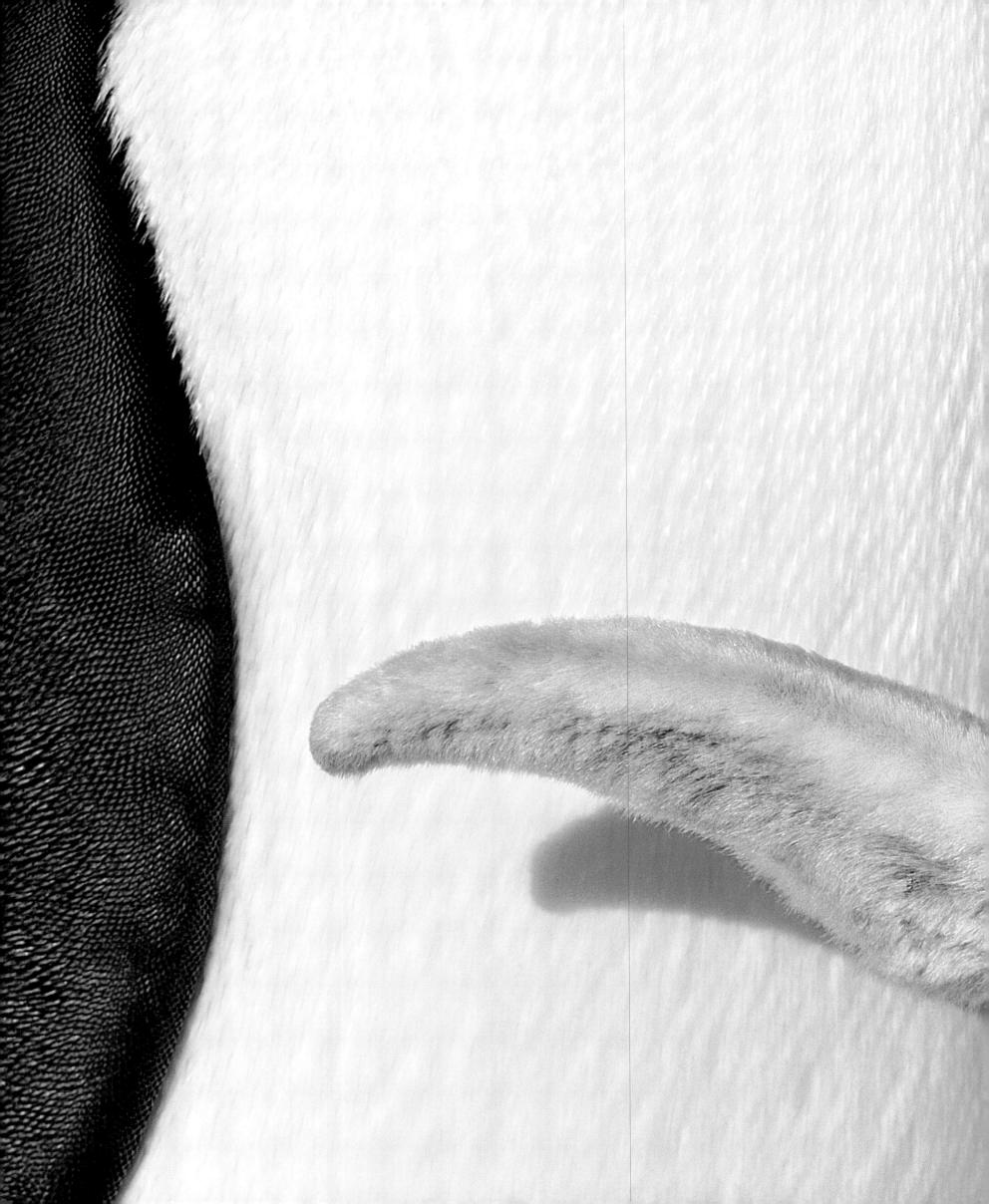

Although strictly a summer breeder, the tough little Adelie penguin's life cycle is also noteworthy. Like all penguins it is a true seabird that only comes ashore in the summer to breed. Thriving Adelie colonies exist right down the Ross Sea coast and on Franklin Island, which is a northern neighbor to Ross Island. The most southerly Adelie colony anywhere on the continent is on Ross Island itself, at Cape Royds (77 degrees South), close to where Shackleton built his 1908–09 expedition base.

In the bitterly cold spring days of October the first Adelies emerge from the ocean, having spent the winter resting on ice floes while feeding on the krill swarms abundant in the Ross Sea. By mid to late October they can be seen streaming in towards Cape Royds, skittering across several hundred miles of ice on their bellies to find and occupy the same rudimentary nesting site of pebbles they used the year before. Soon, they are joined by last year's mate and the process of improving the nest (commonly stealing pebbles from a neighbor), mating, and egg-laying begins. The young chicks are extremely vulnerable to the savage southerly storms that sweep up McMurdo Sound. As the surviving chicks grow they become ever more demanding and have a voracious appetite. The parent birds are constantly kept busy foraging for food. The task of returning to the nest through open water only made easier if the sea ice happens to break up. By the end of February the last of the adult penguins have left Cape Royds, and any chicks not fully fledged and ready for a winter at sea are likely to perish.

58 ADELIE PENGUINS (PYGOSCELIS ADELIAE) ABOUT TO RETURN TO THE ROSS SEA IN SEARCH OF FOOD. THESE ADELIES ARE AT CAPE ROYDS, ROSS ISLAND.

58-59 A STRONG SOUTHERLY WIND BLOWING OFF THE ROSS ICE SHELF IS PUSHING PACK ICE IN MCMURDO SOUND NORTHWARDS INTO THE HEART OF THE ROSS SEA.

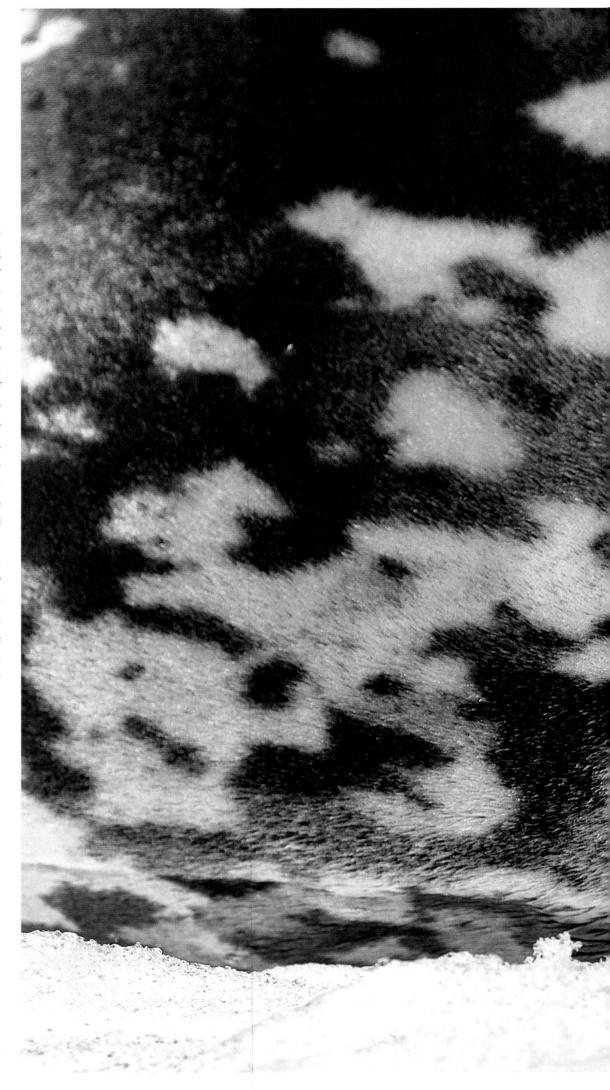

Perhaps the most remarkable creature to inhabit the Ross Sea is the Weddell seal, the most southerly living mammal on Earth. Because they spend the entire winter around Ross Island and along the Ross Sea coast, it is imperative that they keep their breathing holes open through the sea ice by gnawing away at the holes' edges with their strong teeth. The Weddells give birth to their gorgeous silky grey pups in early October, the coldest time of year in Antarctica (the lowest temperature recorded in this part of coastal Antarctica was -65°F/-54°C at Scott base, New Zealand's science base on Ross Island). The pups grow quickly, suckling on a fat-rich milk. The adult Weddell seal as an astounding ability to collapse its lungs and retain oxygen in its blood, enabling it to dive to depths of 1,900 ft (600 m) in McMurdo Sound to locate (in total darkness under the ice) and catch its main prey, bottom-dwelling Mawson cod weighing 110–130 pounds (50–80 kg).

The Ross Sea has long been a hunting ground for Japanese whalers chasing the schools of minke whales, but now fishing fleets come south each summer to catch the lucrative Mawson cod, also know as the Antarctic toothfish. Appropriate management of these fisheries is testing the signatories to the Antarctic Treaty, in particular the governments of New Zealand and Australia that have the protection of the Ross Sea closest to their hearts.

60-61 WEDDELL SEALS (LEPTONYCHOTES WEDDELLII) ARE THE MOST SOUTHERLY MAMMALS IN ANTARCTICA. THEY GIVE BIRTH TO THEIR PUPS IN THE SPRING ON THE SEA ICE AROUND ROSS ISLAND AT 77 DEGREES SOUTH.

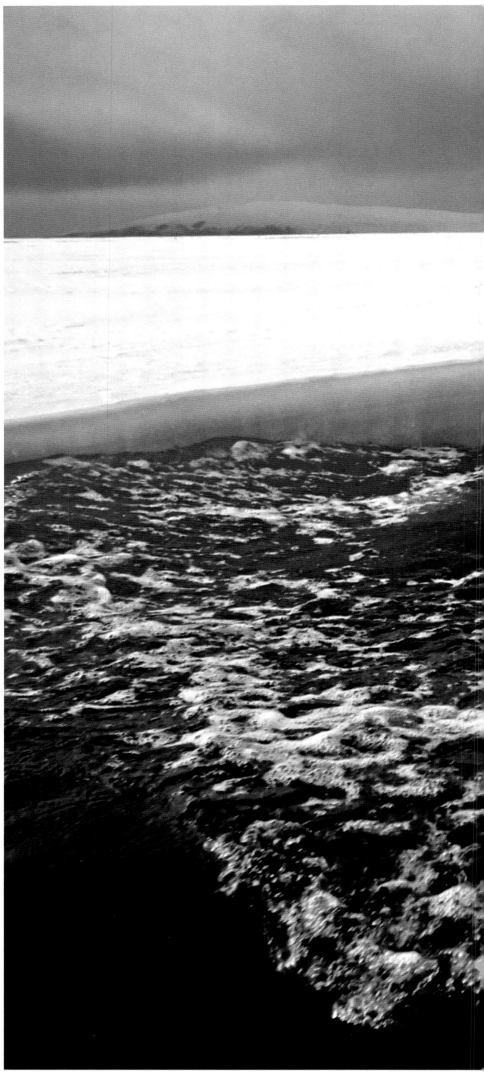

62 AN ANTARCTIC MINKE WHALE (BALAENOPTERA BONAERENSIS) SURFACES IN A POOL OF OPEN WATER IN MCMURDO SOUND. MINKES OFTEN TRAVEL IN LARGE PODS WHILE SEARCHING FOR PLANKTON IN THE PACK ICE.

62-63 KILLER WHALES OR ORCAS (ORCINUS ORCA) ARE THE MOST POWERFUL AND FEARED PREDATORS IN ANTARCTICA. SEALS AND PENGUINS ARE THEIR MAIN PREY. THIS POD OF ORCAS IS SWIMMING FAST THROUGH SEA ICE DOWN A CHANNEL IN MCMURDO SOUND IN THE SOUTHERNMOST PART OF THE ROSS SEA.

64-65 AN ICEBREAKER IN MCMURDO SOUND CARVES A CHANNEL THROUGH THE LARGE FLOES OF PACK ICE AS IT HEADS TOWARDS THE U.S. AND NEW ZEALAND SCIENCE BASES ON ROSS ISLAND.

East
Antarctica

66-67 A WAVE CLOUD OF MIST IS LIT UP AT DAWN AS ITS SPILLS OVER THE EDGE OF THE LAMBERT GLACIER. THE LAMBERT IS 62 MILES (100 KM) WIDE AND 250 MILES (400 KM) LONG, AND IS THE LARGEST GLACIER IN THE WORLD.

67 TOP A NEAR FULL MOON RISES OVER ICEBERGS TRAPPED IN THE SEA ICE OFF THE COAST OF EAST ANTARCTICA.

67 BOTTOM A LONE EMPEROR PENGUIN (APTENODYTES FORSTERI) CROSSES THE PACK ICE TOWARDS HIS COLONY.

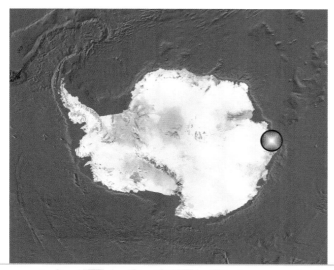

In terms of isolation from humanity, Antartica's most remote coastline lies along the fringe of the West Antarctic Ice Sheet, linking Marie Byrd Land with Ellsworth Land. However, it is hard to find a more forbidding, least-known and seldom-visited coast than the one that runs along the extremity of East Antarctica. This ice-locked landscape, with the East Antarctic Ice Sheet towering above it, is a staggering 3,700 miles (6,000 km) long and is commonly called "deep Antarctica" or, jokingly, the "the far side." East Antarctica is the most hostile, probably the coldest, and certainly the windiest part of maritime Antarctica.

East Antarctica begins at Cape Adare, North Victoria Land, on the edge of the Ross Sea and runs in a single mighty sweep underneath Australia and the South Indian Ocean all the way to Dronning Maud Land at the entrance to the Weddell Sea. In between lies a stretch of coast so extensive that the explorers and scientists who first came here in the late 1800s and early 1900s needed to give separate names to the various sections so they could make sense of their geographical descriptions and sketch maps. From names such as Oates Land, Terre Adelie Land, Wilkes Land, Wilhelm II Land, and Dronning Maud Land, you gain a sense of the British, Australian, American, German, and Norwegian involvement during the so-called Heroic Era.

The voyages and discoveries along this coast span a complex piece of Antarctic history that does not concern us here, however, it is important to know that today there are numerous science bases being operated in East Antarctica. France, Australia, India, China, South Africa, Germany, Japan, Norway, and Russia all have a major presence along this coast. To maintain a year-round presence in this part of Antarctica it is necessary to engage in a complex and costly supply chain. Every year, ice-strengthened ships and ski-equipped aircraft must do battle with the vagaries of the Southern Ocean's weather to bring fuel and food supplies to the coastal stations. They are only able to operate in a narrow window during summer months when the sea ice may relent for a few weeks.

Although the Antarctic Treaty of 1959/60 has effectively frozen any territorial claims, Australia and Norway both have historical territorial rights to most of East Antarctica, with France claiming a tiny pie-shaped sliver that runs all the way inland to the Geographic South Pole from its Terre Adelie Land coast. The South Magnetic Pole lay onshore in George V Land when it was first reached by members of Shackleton's 1908–09 expedition to Ross Island, however, because the magnetic poles "wander" at both ends of the Earth, the South Magnetic Pole is now located at sea off the French base Dumont d'Urville.

68-69 A TABULAR ICEBERG THAT HAS CALVED FROM THE AMERY
ICE SHELF HAS BEEN TRAPPED ON THE EDGE OF THE SEA ICE
OFF THE COAST OF EAST ANTARCTICA. THIS ICEBERG WILL
GRADUALLY ERODE AND MELT AS IT DRIFTS NORTHWARDS
TOWARDS AUSTRALIA.

70 ADELIE PENGUINS (PYGOSCELIS ADELIAE) RIDE A SMALL,
ERODED ICEBERG OFF THE COAST OF TERRE ADELIE LAND.

71 THE ICEBOUND COAST OF SHIRLEY ISLAND IN THE
WINDMILL ISLANDS, EAST ANTARCTICA, GLINTS IN THE
MIDNIGHT SUN.

72-73 EMPEROR PENGUINS (APTENODYTES FORSTERI) SPLASH THROUGH AN ICY POND, WHILE OTHER ADULT BIRDS STANDING ON THE SEA ICE LOOK ON. THERE ARE SEVERAL EMPEROR COLONIES ALONG THE REMOTE COAST OF EAST ANTARCTICA.

73 AN EMPEROR PENGUIN PROPELS ITSELF OUT OF THE WATER ONTO THE SEA ICE NEAR HIS COLONY.

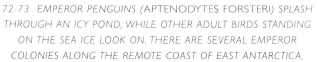

East Antarctica

One of the most impressive parts of East Antarctica is the Lambert Glacier, the largest glacier in the world. The Lambert originates on the Polar Plateau in MacRoberston Land, where 386,000 sq miles (1,000,000 sq km) of ice drains down through the edge of the Prince Charles Mountains to form the gigantic Amery Ice Shelf, which meets the sea. Only discovered in 1947 during aerial mapping flights, the Lambert is 62 miles (100 km) wide and 250 miles (400 km) long (extending for another 190 miles (300 km) as it merges with the Amery Ice Shelf). It is a staggering 8,200 ft (2,500 m) deep with some parts of the ice flowing at 3,900 ft (1,200 m) per year. As the movement is relentless and pressure builds, huge tabular icebergs snap off the Amery to float out into Prydz Bay near the Australian Davis Station.

The East Antarctic Ice Sheet consists of a series of massive ice domes which in places are over 16,400 ft (5,000 m) thick. Crucially for East Antarctica, the barren and essentially lifeless Polar Plateau extends very close to the coast, thereby creating a major height difference in the space of just a few miles. This means that cold, dense, gravity-driven air masses flow steadily down from altitude on the Polar Plateau to blast and chill the entire East Antarctic coastline. These katabatic winds, as they are called, are extremely powerful, affecting wildlife and any people working onshore or steering a ship in the vicinity. Katabatic winds seemingly start up out of nowhere, even when the sky is completely clear. The weather can change from a dead calm to a raging storm in minutes, potentially placing the unwary in a life-threatening situation. Then, in an instant, the wind can drop to an eerie calm again.

Wind is such a powerful force in Antarctica that it can reduce a hardened person to tears of rage and frustration or, dangerously, to complete mental and physical exhaustion. The Australian geologist Douglas Mawson found this out to his cost during his 1911–14 expedition, when he made the mistake of building his wooden hut at Commonwealth Bay in East Antarctica. Over the first year the wind averaged 50 mph (80 km/h), occasionally gusting to 200 mph (320 km/h). The average wind speed for every hour of every day during May was 60 mph (98 km/h), and on May 15 the wind averaged 90 mph (145 km/h) for 24 hours. Mawson's sledging journeys towards the South Magnetic Pole are legendary, but, perhaps more famously, his headquarters became known as "The Home of the Blizzard."

76-77 THE MIDNIGHT SUN LIGHTS UP THE EDGES OF BROKEN ICE FLOES AT EDWARD VIII BAY, KEMP COAST, EAST ANTARCTICA.

78-79 A LOW SUMMER SUN LIGHTS UP THE EDGES OF A TABULAR ICEBERG ADRIFT OFF THE COAST OF EAST ANTARCTICA. THE SURFACE OF THE ICEBERG IS SHATTERED INTO A MAZE OF CREVASSES.

80-81 STORM CLOUDS GATHER OVER AN ICEBERG TRAPPED IN THE PACK ICE NEAR THE COAST OF EAST ANTARCTICA.

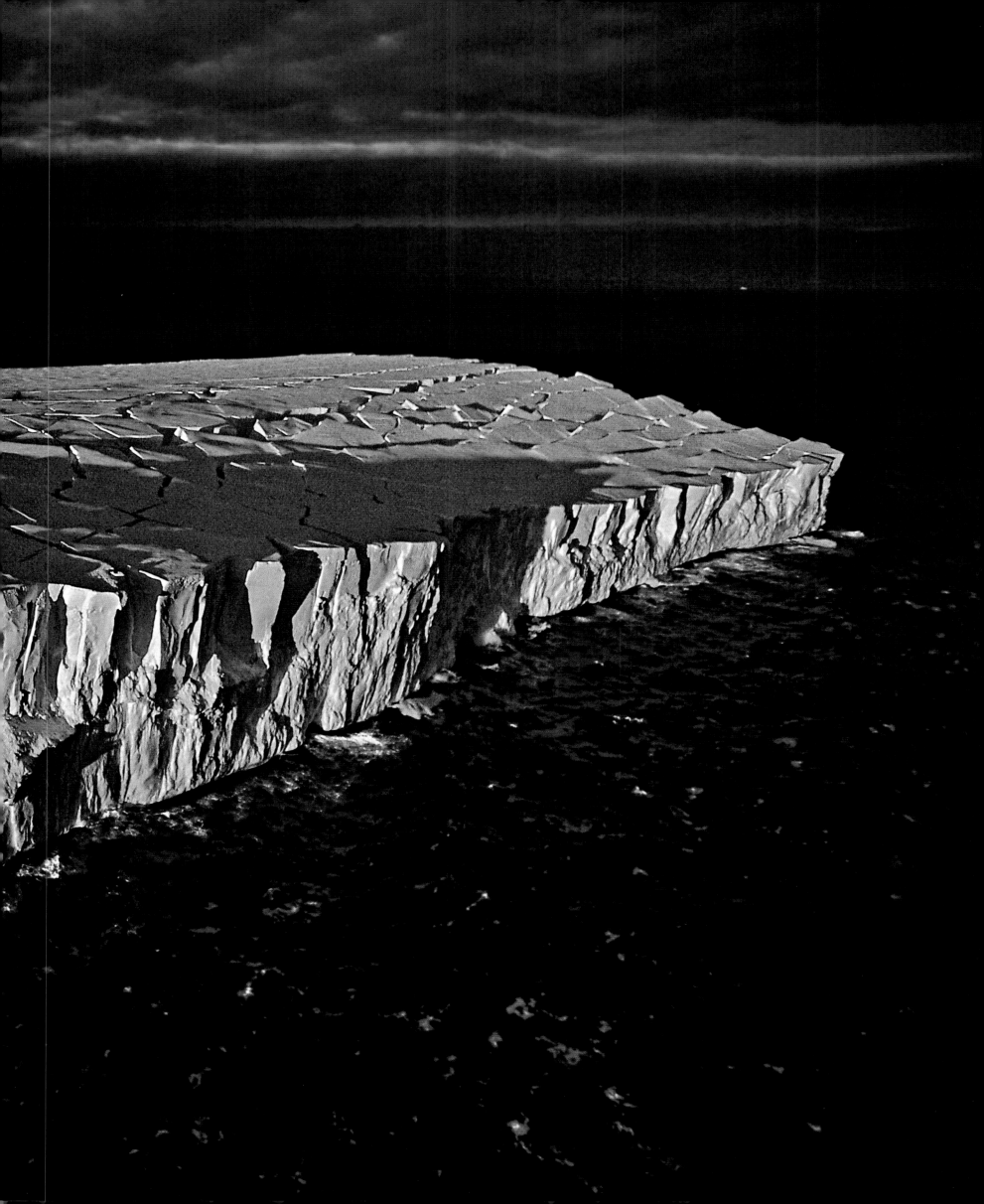

East
Antarctica

82 AND 82-83 DURING THE LONG COLD AND DARK WINTER MONTHS, THE EMPEROR PENGUINS (APTENODYTES FORSTERI) HUDDLE TOGETHER TO STAY WARM AND PROTECT EACH OTHER FROM THE WIND. THE HUDDLE CONSTANTLY MOVES WITH PENGUINS ON THE OUTSIDE GRADUALLY SHUFFLING INTO THE CENTER. THE AUSTER COLONY IS NEAR THE MAWSON RESEARCH BASE IN AUSTRALIAN ANTARCTIC TERRITORY.

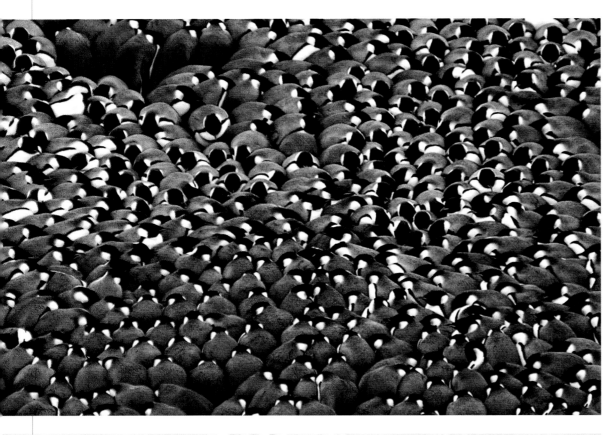

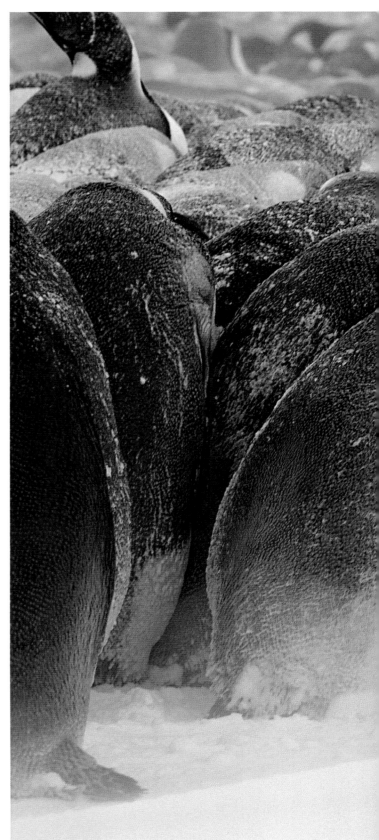

Wildlife is affected by wind too. In the summer, when Adelie penguins are ashore during the short breeding season, an entire generation of chicks can be wiped out when the colony is hit by a windstorm. Unlike Adelies, at least emperor penguins don't build nests on open rocky ground, thereby gaining some wind protection when they form colonies on the sea ice in the lee of ice cliffs or icebergs that are stranded by being frozen into the sea ice. Even so, hundreds of emperors need to huddle together during the worst winter blizzards to gain some warmth and protection against the onslaught of blasting powder snow. The adult emperors take it in turns to

be on the outside of the huddle, jostling the others to the inside in what turns into a constantly shuffling mass of birds.

There are quite a few emperor colonies along the East Antarctic coastline. Most notably the Auster colony near Australia's Mawson Station and another close to France's base, Dumont d'Urville in Terre Adelie Land. The French navigator, Dumont d'Urville, made a superb exploratory voyage to this part of Antarctica in 1840, landing at Point Geologie, not far from the present-day base named after him. It was here that he gave the classic black and white penguin its name, Adelie, after his wife.

Terre Adelie Land is famous, too, because here, on small islands near the French base, are the most southerly colonies of breeding petrels, including the gorgeous pure white snow petrel. In remarkable displays of flying and navigation, snow petrels and Antarctic petrels have been known to fly inland for up to 125 miles (200 km) to establish a nesting colony among the weathered rocks of outcrops and nunataks.

East Antarctica is an enormous icescape of near total wilderness, covering more than half of the entire continent, with a rich diversity of bird and animal life clustered around its coastal fringe. In a few places, too, mosses and lichens cling to life on wind-scoured rock outcrops. There are no higher plants here at all. All the seals and penguins use their bulk and fat layers as some degree of protection against the elements. For many these are the typical, iconic Antarctic creatures, however, for me the snow petrel is the star of the show. Tiny and vulnerable to the worst the continent can throw at them, the snow petrel with its plucky flying skills exhibits the true "spirit of the Antarctic."

Throughout Antarctica there are no national parks or reserves in the conventional sense. There are, however, places and sites designated as Specially Protected Areas or Sites of Special Scientific Interest, and East Antarctica contains many of these special areas. Each of these has very specific and strict management regulations that help protect them from human impact. It is vital that these unique environments remain almost totally untouched for future generations to study, to wonder at, or, for the many of us who will never go to Antarctica, to know that they are simply there in a pristine state.

84-85 A CAPE OR PINTADO PETREL (DAPTION CAPENSE) IN FLIGHT OVER THE SOUTHERN OCEAN. THERE ARE SEVERAL SPECIES OF PETRELS THAT BREED IN THE OFFSHORE ISLANDS OF EAST ANTARCTICA. THE SNOW PETREL (PAGODROMA NIVEA) SOMETIMES FLIES INLAND FOR UP TO 125 MILES (200 KM) TO ESTABLISH ITS NESTING COLONIES.

86-87 IN THE SPRING THE SOUTHERN OCEAN IS ALMOST TOTALLY COVERED WITH FLOES OF SEA ICE, TRAPPING THE MANY TABULAR ICEBERGS THAT BREAK OFF THE GIANT GLACIERS OF EAST ANTARCTICA.

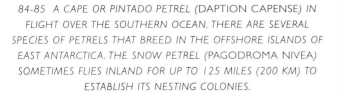

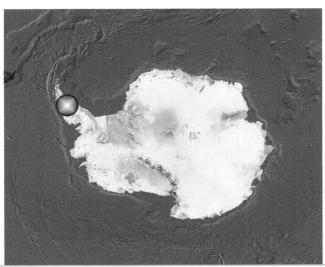

88 TOP A MOUNTAIN PEAK ON WIENCKE ISLAND IS TYPICAL OF THE MANY BEAUTIFUL PEAKS OF THE ANTARCTIC PENINSULA.

88-89 PEAKS ON THE SPINE OF THE ANTARCTICA PENINSULA GLISTEN THROUGH BROKEN CLOUD ABOVE GERLACHE STRAIT.

89 A TYPICAL ALPINE PEAK ON THE ANTARCTIC PENINSULA, MT. SCOTT RISES THROUGH THE CLOUDS AT THE SOUTHERN END OF THE FAMOUS LEMAIRE CHANNEL. MT. SCOTT HAS BEEN CLIMBED A FEW TIMES BY GROUPS FROM NEARBY RESEARCH STATIONS, YACHTS, OR CRUISE SHIPS.

The Antarctic Peninsula

90-91 PERFECT CALM AT SUNRISE IN THE EREBUS AND TERROR GULF OFF THE TIP OF THE ANTARCTIC PENINSULA.

The Antarctic Peninsula is a curved 620-mile (1,000-km) long finger of heavily glaciated mountainous terrain that is studded with beautiful peaks, some of which rise to over 9,800 ft (3,000 m). Geologically, the Antarctic Peninsula is an extension of the massive Andean mountain chain and, like the Andes with its prominent volcanoes, there is active volcanism on Deception Island just off the northern tip of the Peninsula. Some 600 nautical miles (690 miles) beyond the South American continent and due south of Cape Horn, the Peninsula stretches from the ice-choked waters of Hope Bay at 63 degrees South all the way to the edge of Antarctica's Polar Plateau at 74 degrees South. Between the two lies Drake Passage, a tempestuous body of Southern Ocean water that is funneled through this narrow gap between the Pacific and the South Atlantic oceans.

The greater part of the Antarctic Peninsula lies north of the Antarctic Circle and is therefore comparatively mild by Antarctic standards. It is commonly called the "banana belt" because summer temperatures from December to March can climb to 57°F (14°C). Rain is now not uncommon. As the monitoring of global warming becomes more refined, it has been noted that temperatures on the Antarctic Peninsula are warming up faster than anywhere else on the planet, with an average rise of nearly 2°C. At the southern extremities of the Antarctic Peninsula seven ice shelves and major glacier systems are now in various stages of collapse, which are dramatic indicators perhaps of the significant changes that are going to occur in the polar regions.

There is more ice-free land on the Antarctic Peninsula than anywhere else on the continent's coastal fringe, so it is here, sustained by the food-rich seas, that much of Antarctica's wildlife is concentrated. Here, also, since the 1940s at least 15 national Antarctic scientific projects have established year-round bases clustered on the rocky foreshores of the Peninsula and its off-lying islands. Despite the strict environmental and wildlife protection measures of the Antarctic Treaty, the proliferation of permanent installations, the increase in support staff, and the greater numbers of ship and aircraft movements have all impacted to some degree on the breeding colonies of penguins and seabirds and on the delicate plantlife. The number of tourist cruise ships has also dramatically increased in the past 20 years, largely due to the ease of access to the relatively ice-free Antarctic Peninsula from South American ports. Tourism is also causing concern over its cumulative impact on the environment and wildlife through repeated visits to vulnerable sites.

The first land to be sighted after crossing Drake Passage is usually part of the island group known as the South Shetlands. The low-lying, almost subantarctic King George Island, the largest of the South Shetlands, is renowned for the richness of its moss and lichen growth. Because of its accessibility and well-protected natural harbors, it is on King George that many nations have built their research stations. Frequently shrouded in mist, King George is in dramatic contrast to the more glaciated Livingston Island with its elegant alpine peaks. Nearby, glistening Mt. Foster (6,906 ft/2,105 m) is the highest peak on Smith Island and a formidable mountaineering challenge that has been successfully climbed only once, in 1996.

The Antarctic Peninsula

Due South of Livingston Island lies the enigmatic volcano of Deception Island. It is possible to sail a vessel through a narrow gap in the caldera wall, known as Neptune's Bellows, to land on beaches of steaming black scoria. The last major eruption at Deception was in 1969, and as with most active volcanoes there is evidence of near constant and highly unpredictable changes as beaches rise or sink and vigorous erosion scours out gullies at the derelict whaling station at Whaler's Bay. It is from this beach, in 1928, that the Australian pioneer Sir Hubert Wilkins made the first fixed-wing flight in Antarctica. At the far end of the caldera, at Pendulum Cove, it is just possible to swim or at least relax in the narrow strip of thermally heated water.

At Baily Head, on the outside of Deception, a large, steep-fronted glacier flows right down onto a jet-black beach. The ice is impregnated with layer upon layer of ash that has become contorted into wild zebra-striped swirls. Beneath this surreal backdrop hordes of courageous chinstrap penguins crash in through the surf to stand and preen themselves or raucously squawk at each other. Gathering courage for the task ahead, they jauntily start a "Chaplinesque" waddle across the beach to commence the arduous steep climb up to their chicks, which are perched in cliff-top nests on the natural amphitheatre behind the glacier.

Remote and well protected by powerful currents and strong ocean swells, Elephant Island is the easternmost of the South Shetlands group. The large, jagged island was made famous in 1916 after Shackleton's *Endurance* crew was stranded there at Point Wild. It was from here that the lifeboat, *James Caird*, set sail for South Georgia so that Shackleton could raise the alarm. All the islands of the South Shetlands are home to numerous chinstrap and gentoo penguin colonies as well as the breeding sites for other seabirds, such as shags, sheathbills, and various species of petrels. However, it was the incredible numbers of fur seals that first put the islands on the map. British and American sealers based themselves here in the early 1800s to plunder a rich harvest of seal pelts. They were often hostile to each other due to the competitive and lucrative nature of the trade. The abundant and slow-moving elephant seals were also taken for the oil in their blubber.

Leaving the South Shetlands behind, the 70-mile (112-km) wide Bransfield Strait has to be crossed before the northernmost tip of the Antarctic Peninsula is reached. Massive tabular icebergs are now encountered as they are swept westwards out of the Weddell Sea through Antarctic Sound. There is also a dramatic drop in the temperature as freezing katabatic winds spill down from the peaks above Hope Bay. One of the mountains, Mt. Flora, is a Specially Protected Area due to the many plant fossils found there, which provide evidence of an earlier epoch when Antarctica was much warmer. The scenery is now distinctly polar, with heavier pack ice jamming up the bays, bigger glaciers flowing down into the sea, and higher, snow-draped peaks. This is the start of a mighty continent that is twice the size of Australia.

It is possible to cross Antarctic Sound and enter the Weddell Sea on the eastern side of the Antarctic Peninsula, however, it is common to have a ship's passage blocked by heavy pack ice. Icebergs are also a significant threat as they can move independently through the pack ice, pushed along by strong currents and wind.

This is a very harsh environment and is no place for an inexperienced captain or a vessel that is not properly strengthened to withstand ice.

92 CHINSTRAP PENGUINS (PYGOSCELIS ANTARCTICUS)
LANDING ON THE BLACK VOLCANIC BEACH AT BAILY HEAD,
DECEPTION ISLAND.

92-93 DECEPTION ISLAND IS AN ACTIVE VOLCANO IN THE SOUTH
SHETLANDS GROUP NEAR THE ANTARCTIC PENINSULA.

93 TOP THE CHINSTRAP PENGUIN COLONY COVERS BAILY HEAD,
DECEPTION ISLAND.

94-95 THE CHINSTRAP COLONY ON HALF MOON ISLAND, SOUTH
SHETLAND ISLANDS, IS SHELTERED BY THE JAGGED REMNANTS OF
AN OLD VOLCANO.

The Antarctic
Peninsula

96-97 AN IMPERIAL OR BLUE-EYED
SHAG (PHALACROCORAX ATRICEPS)
ON ITS NEST, WIENCKE ISLAND.

97 IMPERIAL SHAGS IN A MUTUAL
PREENING DISPLAY.

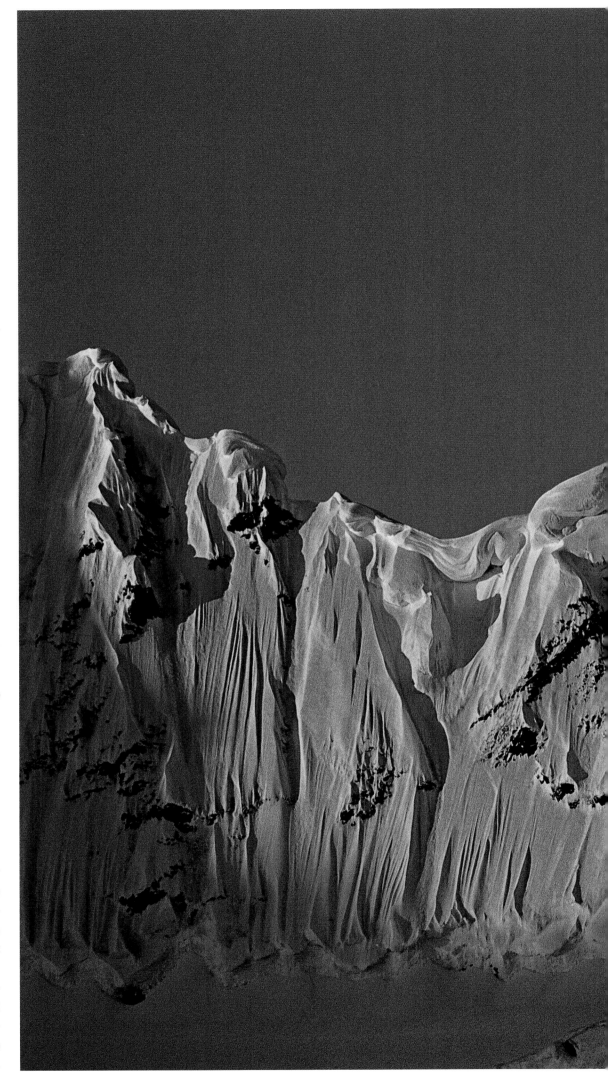

98-99 SUNSET LIGHTS UP THE HIGHEST SUMMITS ON WIENCKE ISLAND.

100-101 MIRROR-CALM REFLECTIONS ARE COMMON IN THE LEMAIRE CHANNEL, A NARROW PASSAGE BETWEEN BOOTH ISLAND AND THE ANTARCTIC PENINSULA.

It is more usual to voyage down the western side of the Antarctic Peninsula and cruise past the islands of Brabant and Anvers in the relatively protected, more ice-free waters of Gerlache Strait. The 9,800-ft (3,000-m) ice peak of Mt. Francais, the highest point on Anvers Island, glows a soft pastel pink during the long, lingering sunsets. Even this far north on the Antarctic Peninsula, there is essentially continuous daylight during the midsummer months from December to February.

Further south on the Antarctic Peninsula the geography becomes more complex with a myriad of islands, channels, and seemingly secret passageways gradually opening up. It simply becomes more and more beautiful, with countless unnamed, unclimbed peaks bristling along the spine of the Peninsula, and with contorted, heavily crevassed glaciers, many of which have never been crossed. Cruising through the narrow and justly famous Lemaire Channel it is awe-inspiring to stand on deck and gaze upward at the massive rock faces that are laced with precarious ice cliffs and overhanging ice mushrooms called cornices. Often there is a perfect mirror-image reflection of the channel gleaming in the water ahead of the ship. Then, with Lemaire now in the wake, the horizon is filled once again with a panorama of wonderful mountains. Navigation southward to Adelaide Island and enormous Marguerite Bay near the base of the Antarctic Peninsula becomes trickier as more and more icebergs are encountered and the pack ice gets denser, often completely covering the sea even in midsummer.

Many of the floes are dotted with pods of snoozing, tawny-colored crabeater seals, thought to be the most numerous mammal on the planet after humans. There are no crabs in the Antarctic, but the name given to the species by early explorers has stuck. Crabeaters prefer to inhabit the pack ice and rarely come ashore even to breed. They primarily eat the shrimp-like krill and their dog-like snout has specially shaped teeth that interlock to help filter out mouthfuls of the crustacean from the sea water. Often crabeaters' pelts are lacerated with scars which are the result of orca attacks. The bulkier, silver speckled Weddell seal is also found on the Antarctic Peninsula, as is the more solitary and ferocious leopard seal which often patrols off the edge of a penguin colony in the hope of snapping up a meal.

102 A GENTOO PENGUIN CHICK (PYGOSCELIS PAPUA) WITH ITS CORRUGATED TONGUE ADAPTED FOR CATCHING KRILL OR SQUID.

102-103 GENTOO PENGUIN COLONIES ARE COMMONLY FOUND ON MANY OF THE ISLANDS ON THE WESTERN SIDE OF THE ANTARCTIC PENINSULA. THEY PREFER BARE ROCKY WELL-DRAINED AND ICE-FREE LAND TO BUILD THEIR NEST OF STONES.

104 SUNSET IN PARADISE BAY LIGHTS UP SMALL ICE FLOES AND THE MOUNTAINS OF THE ANTARCTIC PENINSULA BEHIND.

104-105 CRABEATER SEALS (LOBODON CARCINOPHAGUS) SNOOZE ON A SMALL ICE FLOE ON A WARM SUMMER'S DAY ON THE ANTARCTIC PENINSULA.

106-107 A LONE GENTOO PENGUIN (PYGOSCELIS PAPUA) APPEARS STRANDED ON THE EDGE OF A BLUE ICEBERG THAT HAS ORIGINATED FROM THE ICE SHELVES IN THE WEDDELL SEA.

108 AN ORCA (KILLER WHALE: ORCINUS ORCA) BREACHING OUT OF THE ICY WATERS OFF THE ANTARCTIC PENINSULA. ORCA ROUTINELY PATROL THE FJORDS AND CHANNELS AROUND THE ANTARCTIC PENINSULA AS THEY HUNT FOR SEALS AND PENGUINS AMONG THE ICE FLOES.

108-109 A HUMPBACK WHALE (MEGAPTERA NOVAEANGLIAE) SWIMS BESIDE AN ICEBERG. HUMPBACKS ARE INCREASINGLY COMMON AROUND THE ANTARCTIC PENINSULA NOW THAT THE WHALING ERA IS OVER.

110-111 THE LEOPARD SEAL (HYDRURGA LEPTONYX) IS THE MOST FEARED PREDATOR IN ANTARCTICA. THEY COMMONLY PATROL THE WATERS NEAR PENGUIN COLONIES OR ATTACK CRABEATER SEALS RESTING ON ICE FLOES.

The three species of "bristletail" penguins, the Adelie (named after the French explorer Dumont d'Urville's wife), the gentoo, and the chinstrap all have thriving colonies on the Peninsula. There is only one small breeding colony of emperor penguins, however, and that is a long way south on Dion Island just off Adelaide Island. The penguins all have to breed and raise chicks during the brief austral summer months before they return to the sea and the pack ice for the winter. Competition is fierce for snow-free sites with access to pebbles for nest-building. The flooding of eggs out of nests can be a problem during the height of the summer snow melt, so preference is given to well-drained locations. One adult penguin takes its turn sitting on the one or two eggs, while the other is out at sea searching for krill.

This becomes a frenetic near-continuous activity as the plump, down-covered chicks develop a more and more voracious appetite. Now that the shore-based whaling industry has stopped in Antarctica (with only a few Japanese whaling vessels continuing to hunt elsewhere in the Southern Ocean), it is heartening that more and more minke and humpback whales can be seen around the Antarctic Peninsula. The minke, a small fast-swimming whale that likes to inhabit waters around pack ice, and the bigger, seemingly more playful humpback are both filter feeders, consuming vast quantities of krill in a single meal. The Antarctic Peninsula is a place of great physical and spiritual beauty. The sheer scale and grandeur of this wilderness environment deeply affects all who come here. It is very special to gain a sense of insignificance in this vast, near pristine landscape where there are no fences, powerlines, and roads, and where humans maintain only a precarious existence at a few, small scientific facilities clinging to the coast.

112 AN ADELIE PENGUIN (PYGOSCELIS ADELIAE) JUMPS OVER A GAP IN SNOW BOULDERS.

112-113 A TYPICAL SMALL COLONY OF ADELIE PENGUINS ON PETERMANN ISLAND OFF THE COAST OF THE ANTARCTIC PENINSULA. GENTOO PENGUINS AND IMPERIAL SHAGS BREED ON PETERMANN ISLAND AS WELL AS ADELIES.

114-115 ICE-FILLED PARADISE BAY AS THE SUN LIGHTS UP THE HIGHEST SUMMITS ON THE ANTARCTIC PENINSULA.

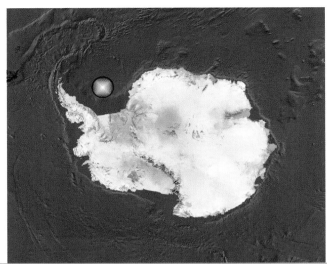

116 TOP THERE ARE SEVERAL EMPEROR PENGUIN (APTENODYTES FORSTERI) COLONIES AT THE SOUTHERN EXTREMITY OF THE WEDDELL SEA, NOTABLY AT ATKA BAY.

116-117 AN AERIAL VIEW OF TABULAR ICEBERGS TRAPPED IN PACK ICE IN THE WEDDELL SEA.

117 LARGE FLOES OF SEA ICE UP TO 16 FT (5 M) THICK GRIND TOGETHER IN THE WEDDELL SEA. ALMOST THE ENTIRE SURFACE OF THE SEA IS COVERED AND IT IS VERY HARD FOR ICE-STRENGTHENED SHIPS TO PENETRATE EVEN DURING MID-SUMMER.

The Weddell Sea

If there is one place that strikes fear and awe into the heart of anyone voyaging to Antarctica it is the Weddell Sea. Ever since 1915 when Sir Ernest Shackleton's ship *Endurance* sank here, after being trapped for months in the heavy, grinding ice floes, the Weddell Sea's reputation has grown, commanding the utmost respect from all mariners. The Weddell is part of the Southern Ocean, yet it is so vast and so formidable in its own right that this great iceberg factory is grandly impressive, the ultimate Antarctic powerhouse. As a polar marine environment of great beauty and wonder the Weddell is only matched by the mighty Ross Sea. In recent years, the sudden collapse of major ice shelves deep in the Weddell Sea has been alarming, harbingers no doubt of the more dramatic effects of climate change yet to come – of global warming on a scale never witnessed before.

The Weddell Sea covers 1.16 million sq miles (3 million sq km) and is some 1,150 miles across at its widest point, stretching from the Coats Land coast all the way to the eastern edge of the Antarctic Peninsula. The Weddell is rarely, if ever, an open sea and is almost always a massive cauldron of heaving ice floes throughout the year. This sea ice, as Shackleton found to his cost, gets swept along in an unstoppable clockwise direction towards the Antarctic Peninsula. The floes can be 6 to 15 ft thick and virtually impenetrable, sometimes even by a modern icebreaker.

It is all the more remarkable, therefore, that as early as 1823 the British captain of a sealing ship, James Weddell, managed to navigate his tiny wooden sailing ships, *Jane* and *Beaufoy*, into a relatively ice-free sea that now bears his name, reaching 74 degrees South. (Weddell originally named his discovery King George IV Sea.) This was 195 miles further south than Captain Cook had managed 50 years before and it would be another 90 years before this latitude was reached again. Weddell had previously been to the South Shetland Islands and on this voyage discovered the South Orkney Islands. Weddell believed that after he broke through the sea-ice barrier he would enter an ocean that went all the way to the Geographic South Pole.

Although this part of Antarctica proved not to have any of the Antarctic fur seals (*Arctocephalus gazella*) that Weddell had hoped for, it does have a significant seal population. Both the Weddell (*Leptonychotes weddelli*) and crabeater seals (*Lobodon carcinophagus*) inhabit these waters. Crabeater seals prefer to live exclusively on the pack ice. Given the size of the Southern Ocean and the difficulty of navigating through the pack ice, it has been near impossible to do an accurate census of crabeaters. It is thought, however, that after humans it is the most numerous mammal on the planet.

There are no crabs in the Antarctic, so when this new seal was given its name by the sealers they were undoubtably confused by the pink marks around its mouth caused by its principal food, krill, or perhaps they spotted the pink-stained faeces left behind on the ice. The crabeater with its dog-like snout has specially adapted interlocking teeth to help strain out the water and while retaining mouthfuls of krill. It has a soft, silvery-brown coat that is often deeply scarred with wounds following encounters with orca. The crabeater is quite gregarious and commonly groups of 10 or 20 can be seen during the summer months snoozing on ice floes. It has no need to come ashore at all, not even to breed as their pups are born in the spring out on the sea ice.

Weddell seal pups, however, are often born ashore or at least on the sea ice closest to the islands around the western fringe of the Weddell Sea, such as Paulet, James Ross, and Snow Hill islands. Leopard seals (*Hydrurga leptonyx*) also frequent the Weddell Sea. Their main prey is Adelie or chinstrap penguins (though they also eat a lot of krill) and they are routinely seen patrolling the shores of the islands during summer months, in the hope of catching an unwary penguin coming or going from its colony.

The most elusive seal of all though is the Ross seal (*Ommatophoca rossi*), which is a brown-haired, thick-necked seal with distinctive dark streaks on its head and shoulders. The Ross seal is solitary, inhabiting the most remote ice floes in the heart of the Weddell Sea. It is also found in the extensive belts of pack ice around the Southern Ocean, such as in deepest East Antarctica.

120 A WEDDELL SEAL (LEPTONYCHOTES WEDDELLII) HAS
BROKEN THROUGH A THIN LAYER OF SEA ICE SO IT CAN
BREATHE. THE SOUTHERNMOST MAMMAL, THE WEDDELL SEAL
CAN DIVE TO DEPTHS OF 1,900 FT (600 M) AS IT HUNTS FOR
FISH ON THE SEA FLOOR.

120-121 A WEDDELL SEAL AND PUP SWIMMING BENEATH
SEA ICE. WEDDELL SEAL PUPS ARE BORN ON THE SEA ICE
IN THE COLD SPRING MONTH OF OCTOBER. THE PUPS GROW
QUICKLY THANKS TO THE MOTHER'S EXTREMELY FAT-RICH MILK
AND THEY MUST BE READY FOR A LIFE IN THE OCEAN IN ONLY
A FEW MONTHS.

The Weddell Sea

122-123 A CRABEATER SEAL (LOBODON CARCINOPHAGUS) YAWNS AS IT LIES ON A SMALL ICEBERG IN THE WEDDELL SEA. CRABEATERS HAVE A DOG-LIKE SNOUT WITH TRICUSPID-SHAPED TEETH THAT INTERLOCK WHEN THE JAW IS CLOSED, ALLOWING SEA WATER TO FILTER OUT AND RETAINING A MOUTHFUL OF KRILL.

123 WEDDELL SEAL PUPS ARE BORN IN THE COLD SPRING MONTHS OF SEPTEMBER AND OCTOBER ON THE EDGE OF THE PACK ICE OR ON ISLANDS ON THE WESTERN SIDE OF THE WEDDELL SEA. BOTH THE ADULTS AND PUPS HAVE A THICK LAYER OF BLUBBER AND A TIGHTLY PACKED LAYER OF FUR ON THEIR PELTS, ENABLING THEM TO STAY WARM EVEN IN THE FIERCEST OF BLIZZARDS.

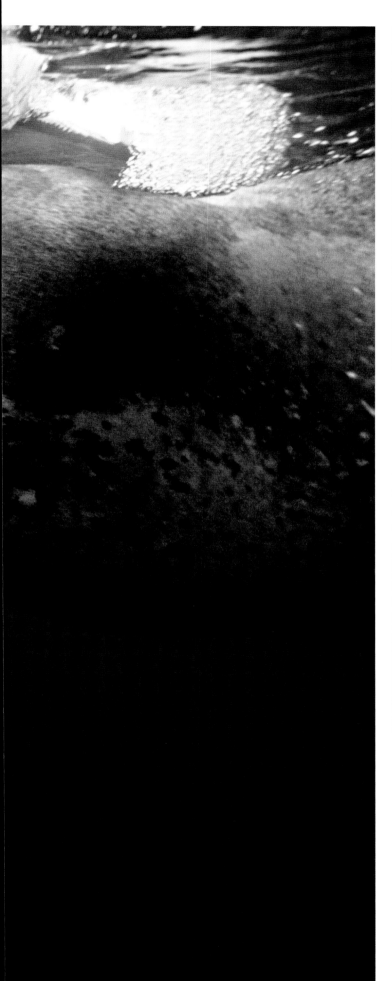

124-125 AND 125 A FEARED PREDATOR, A LEOPARD SEAL
(HYDRURGA LEPTONYX) CATCHES A CHINSTRAP PENGUIN
(PYGOSCELIS ANTARCTICUS) AND PLAYS WITH IT BEFORE
FINALLY KILLING IT AND STRIPPING OFF ITS FEATHERS AND SKIN.

Perhaps the most famous creature found here is the elegant and incredibly stoic emperor penguin, the ultimate polar bird. There are several emperor penguin breeding grounds in the remotest recesses of the Weddell Sea coast, though perhaps the most famous are the Atka Bay and Riiser-Larsen colonies. The emperor does not build a nest, in fact it doesn't even need land to lay its egg, preferring the sea ice to establish its colony. Emperor colonies can consist of several thousand birds and they huddle together for warmth and communal support against the fiercest of winter blizzards, often using the lee of a tabular iceberg that is trapped in the ice for protection from the wind.

Remarkably, after the egg is laid in midwinter, the female transfers the egg to its male partner who incubates and hatches the chick.

The egg is kept warm between the adult bird's scaly feet and its belly feathers. Using his own body reserves, the male feeds and nurtures the chick while the female is at sea hunting for fish and krill. She will return to the colony in the spring to take over duties of feeding the voraciously hungry chick. By now, the male is emaciated from his harrowing and extended role as parent. These are astonishingly tough birds, but a single blizzard can wipe out many hundreds of chicks in a few hours. Life in this freezer is never easy.

126 A RAPIDLY GROWING EMPEROR PENGUIN CHICK (APTENODYTES FORSTERI) CHASES ONE OF ITS PARENTS IN THE HOPE OF BEING FED SOME KRILL.

126-127 BEFORE DIVING BACK INTO THE WEDDELL SEA TO HUNT FOR KRILL, THESE ADELIE PENGUINS (PYGOSCELIS ADELIAE) GLIDE ACROSS AN ICE FLOE ON THEIR BREASTS, PUSHING THEMSELVES ALONG WITH THEIR POWERFUL FLIPPERS.

128-129 *THE EMPEROR PENGUIN (APTENODYTES FORSTERI) IS THE TALLEST, HEAVIEST, AND MOST BEAUTIFUL OF ALL THE PENGUIN SPECIES. THEY HAVE A MOST UNUSUAL BREEDING CYCLE, LAYING AN EGG ON THE BARE ICE DURING WINTER. HERE A PAIR ARE COURTING AT ONE OF THE COLONIES IN THE WEDDELL SEA.*

130-131 TABULAR ICEBERGS THAT HAVE
BROKEN OFF ANTARCTICA'S ICE SHELVES
ARE ERODED BY WAVE ACTION, FORMING
LARGE TUNNELS BEFORE THEY FINALLY
BREAK APART.

132 A LONE ADELIE PENGUIN (PYGOSCELIS ADELIAE) HAS CLAWED ITS WAY UP INTO A ICE CAVE IN A WEATHERED ICEBERG.

133 THE WEDDELL SEA IS FAMOUS FOR BEING THE SOURCE OF STUNNING BLUE ICEBERG SPIRES. WHEN THE ICE IS OLD IT IS HIGHLY COMPRESSED AND SO HAS ALL THE OXYGEN SQUEEZED OUT OF IT, HENCE THE BLUE APPEARANCE.

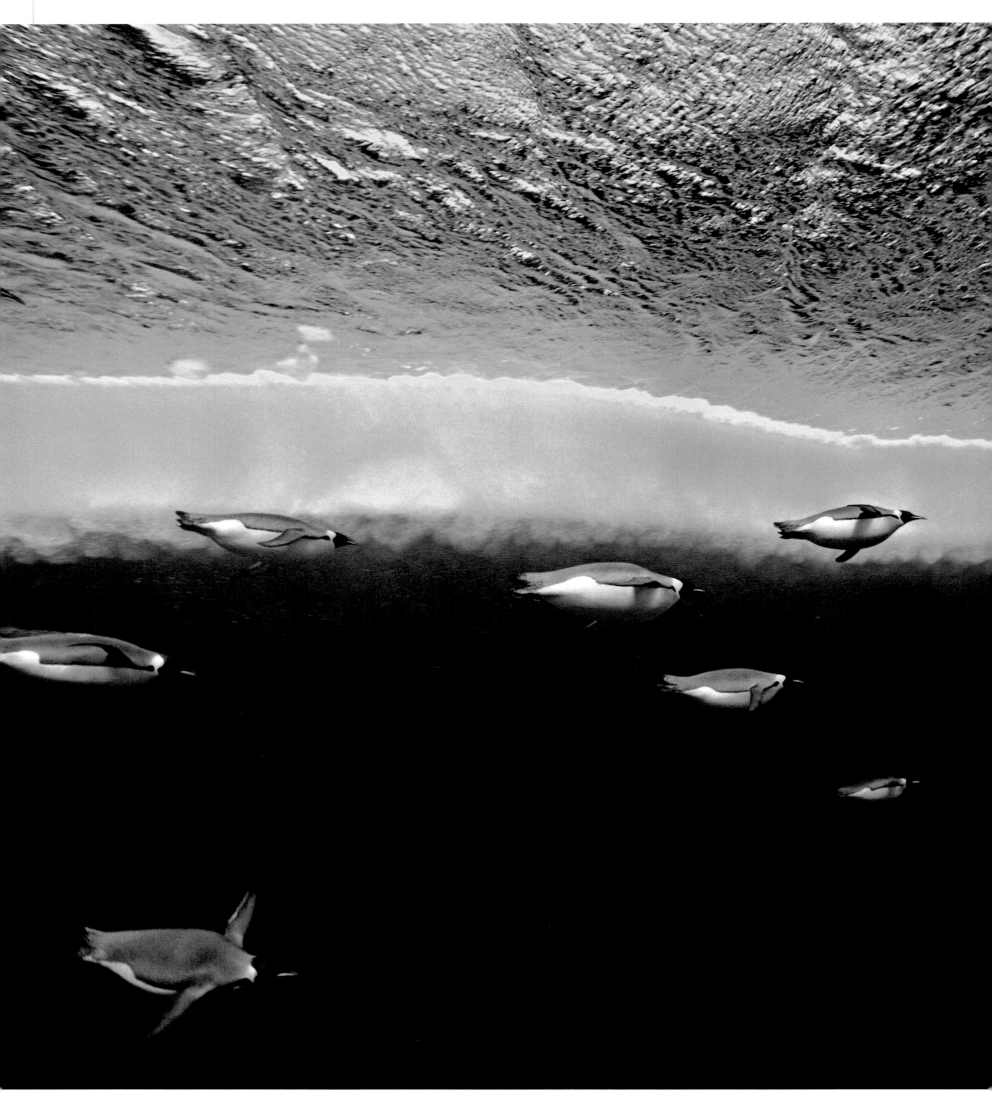

134-135 AND 135 EMPEROR PENGUINS (APTENODYTES FORSTERI) SWIMMING UNDER SEA ICE IN THE WEDDELL SEA. EMPERORS ARE REMARKABLE SWIMMERS AND THEY CAN REACH DEPTHS OF SEVERAL HUNDRED FEET WHEN CHASING KRILL, SQUID, AND FISH.

136-137 A DIVER EXAMINES THE LIFE FORMS THAT EXIST ON THE UNDERSIDE OF SEA ICE IN THE WEDDELL SEA, FINDING SMALL FISH WITH GLYCOPROTEIN (ANTIFREEZE) IN THEIR BLOOD, KRILL, AND STARFISH. A BLUE-GREEN ALGAE ALSO COMMONLY GROWS ON THE ICE.

138-139 OLD ICEBERGS THAT DRIFT NORTHWARDS OUT OF THE WEDDELL SEA ARE OFTEN JADE GREEN OR BLUE DUE TO THEIR HIGHLY COMPRESSED ICE. FREQUENTLY, THEY HAVE LAYERS OF FINE ROCK SEDIMENT TRAPPED WITHIN THEM, CREATING A BEAUTIFUL CHOCOLATE CAKE APPEARANCE.

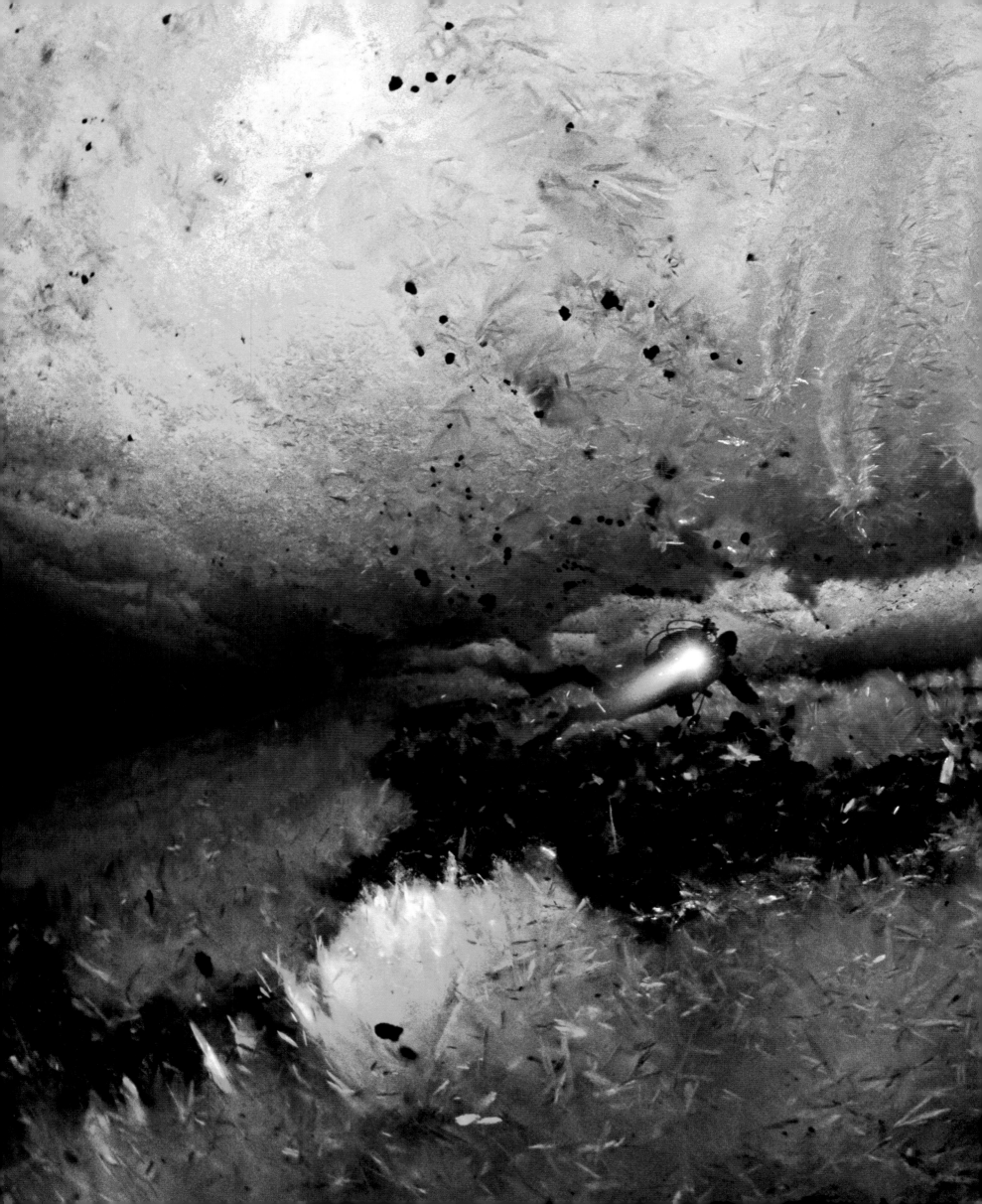

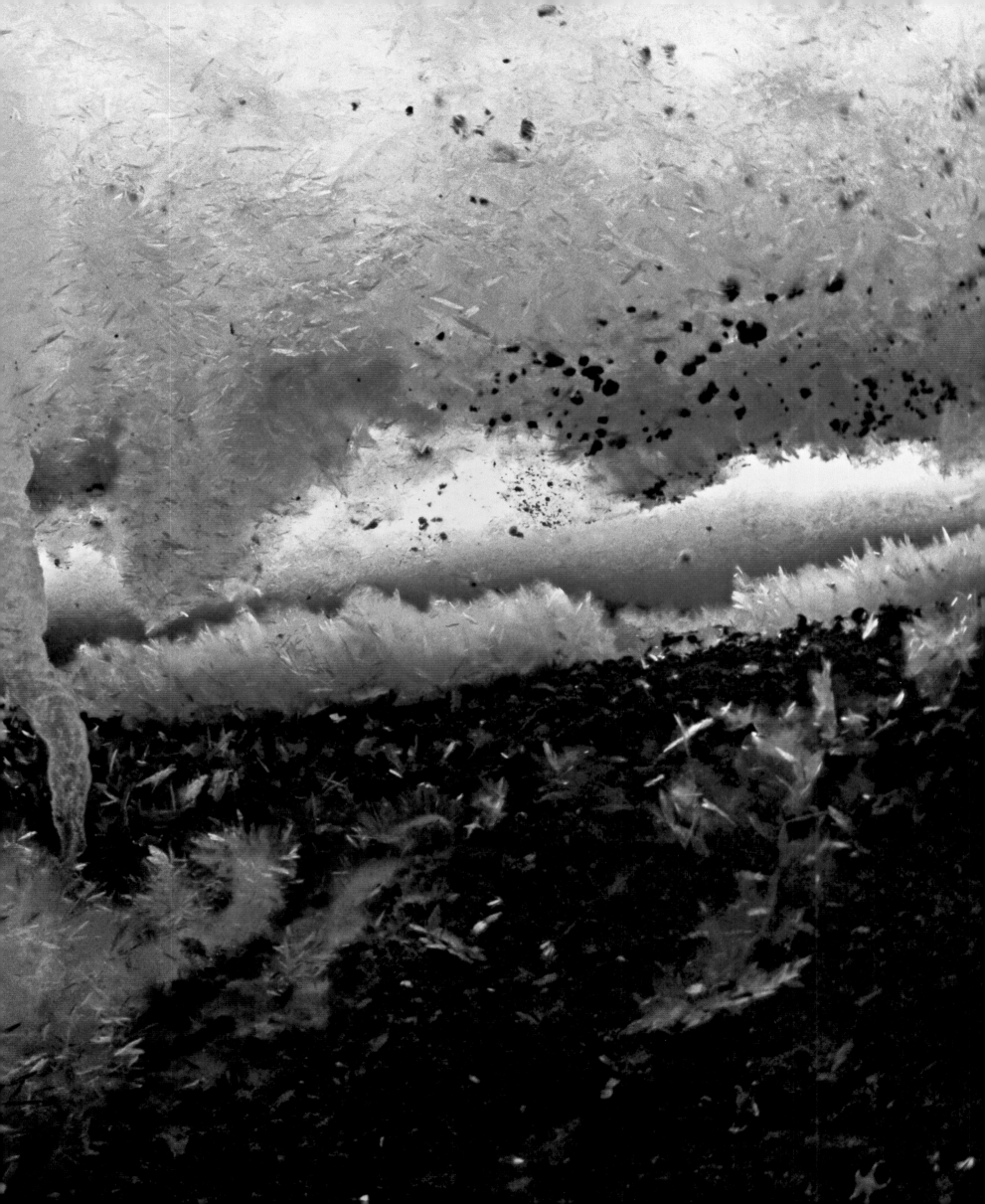

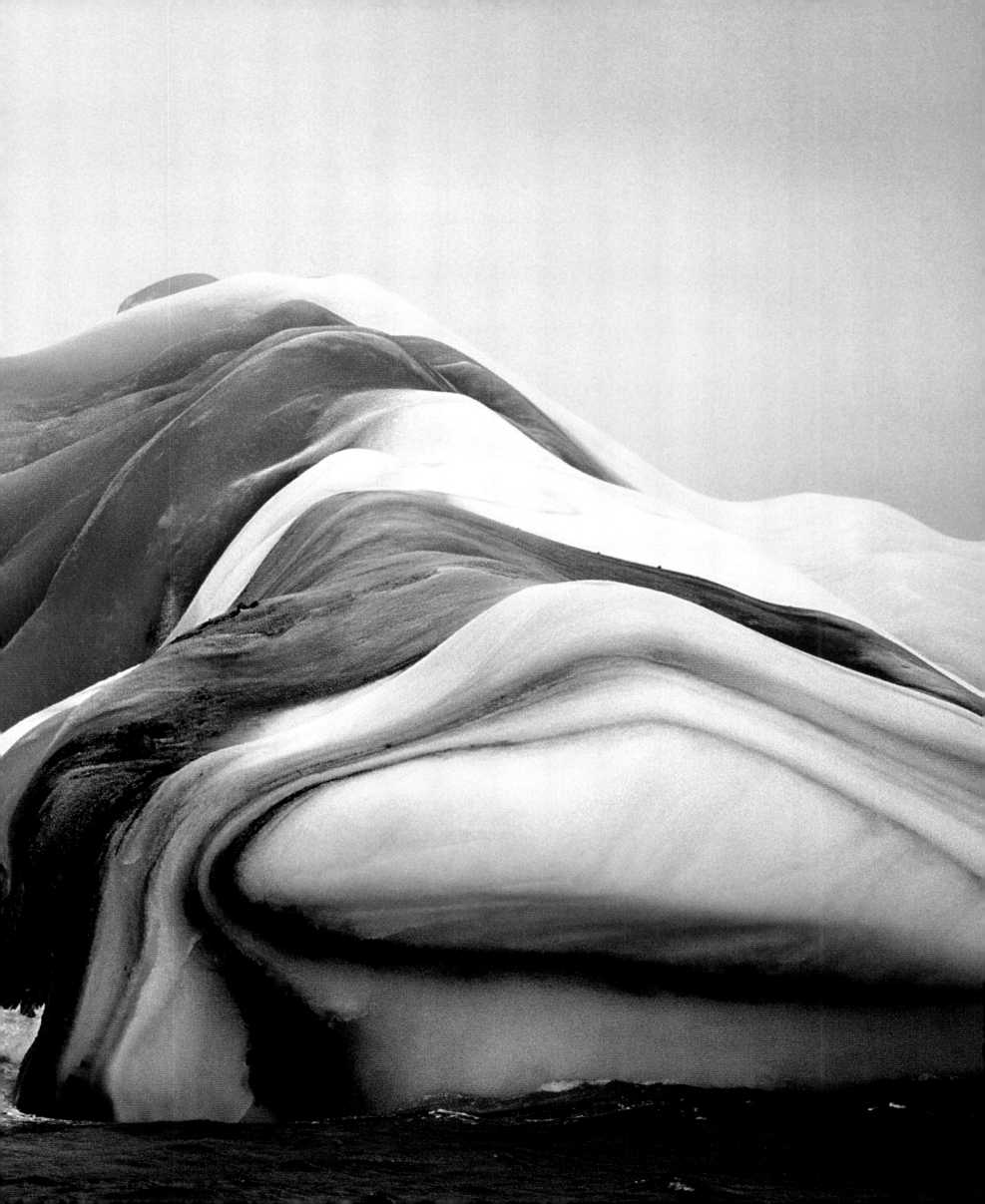

The Filchner-Ronne Ice Shelf is second only in size to the Ross Ice Shelf on the opposite side of the continent. Divided by Berkner Island, the combined area of the Filchner and the larger Ronne ice shelves is 166,000 sq miles (430,000 sq km). As the ice shelf is fed by glaciers that flow from the East Antarctic Ice Sheet, the Filchner-Ronne is continually moving and is being pushed ever seaward. When the shearing stresses exceed the strength of the ice, enormous tabular icebergs split off and calve into the Weddell Sea. In 1998 and again in 2000, icebergs that measured approximately 60 by 20 sq miles (150 by 50 km) broke off and drifted northward into the Weddell before gradually breaking up. Many of these tabular bergs reached Antarctic Sound at the tip of the Antarctic Peninsula. Some even drifted with the currents up to the latitude of the South Orkney Islands and South Georgia before melting. The Filchner-Ronne ice shelf displays the annual layers of snow accumulation much like the growth rings of a tree. These layers have been gradually compressed into ice. At times, bands of sediment, silt, and rock are incorporated into these layers, which can give an iceberg the appearance of a chocolate cake. Iridescent blue icebergs are made of very old ice that has had all the oxygen squeezed out.

In 2002, the Larsen Ice Shelf attached to the eastern side of the Antarctic Peninsula collapsed, which was observed in a dramatic series of satellite images. Thousands of tabular icebergs, covering an area of 1,150 sq miles (3,000 sq km), separated from the continent and calved into the Weddell Sea. Over the next five years at least a further 770 sq miles (2,000 sq km) broke off. This is unprecedented in recorded glaciological history and is attributed to a rapid warming of the climate in the region. The break-up of ice shelves in the Weddell Sea will be monitored closely as scientists continue to try to get a clearer picture of the climate mechanisms at work. With significant warming also occurring in the Arctic, both polar regions will play an increasingly important role in helping scientists to measure the changes in the global climate.

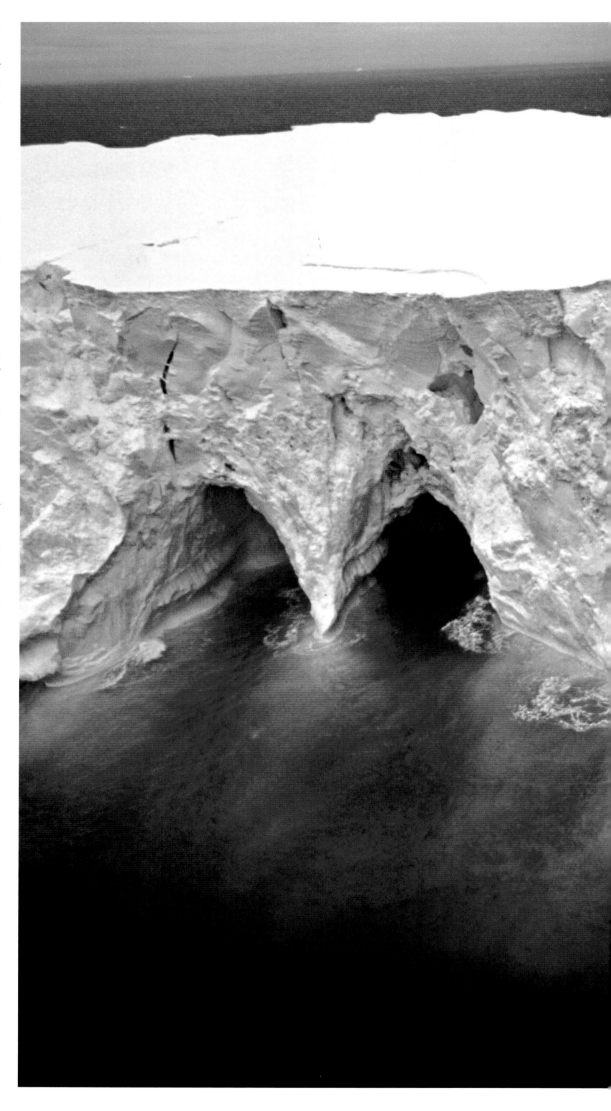

140-141 AN AERIAL VIEW OF AN ICEBERG THAT HAS HAD LARGE CAVES ERODED INTO IT BY WAVE ACTION AS IT DRIFTS NORTHWARDS IN THE WEDDELL SEA.

142-143 AN AERIAL VIEW OF ICEBERGS TRAPPED IN THE PACK ICE OF THE WEDDELL SEA. THE COLLAPSE OF MAJOR GLACIERS AND ICE SHELVES ON THE EDGE OF THE WEDDELL SEA OVER THE LAST DECADE IS ONE OF THE MOST DRAMATIC EXAMPLES OF GLOBAL WARMING EVER WITNESSED.

144-145 ON THE IMMENSE EXPANSES OF ICE IN THE WEDDELL SEA IT IS NOT DIFFICULT TO BUMP INTO COLONIES OF EMPEROR PENGUINS ESPECIALLY DURING THE BREEDING SEASON BETWEEN MARCH AND APRIL. THE EMPEROR PENGUIN REPRODUCES MAINLY ON VAST EXPANSES OF ICE WHICH CAN BE SEVERAL KILOMETERS FROM THE COAST.

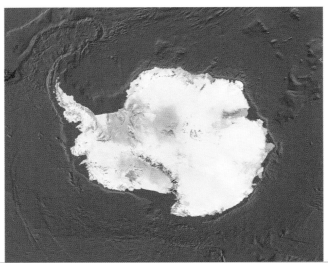

146 TOP AN 80-KNOT STORM FLATTENS THE WAVES IN THE DRAKE PASSAGE, JUST SOUTH OF CAPE HORN. THE DRAKE PASSAGE IS ONLY 600 MILES (1,000 KM) WIDE AND LIES BETWEEN THE ANTARCTIC PENINSULA AND CAPE HORN, A CHILEAN ISLAND OFF THE TIP OF SOUTH AMERICA. THE SOUTHERN OCEAN IS FORCED THROUGH THIS GAP, WHICH OFTEN CREATES STORMY SEAS.

146-147 SOUTHERN OCEAN WAVES SMASH INTO A MASSIVE TABULAR ICEBERG SENDING SPRAY SKYWARD.

The Southern Ocean

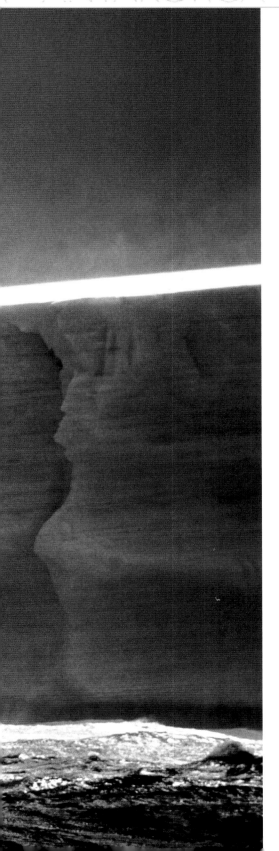

Antarctica is surrounded by the great Southern Ocean, the wildest and least-known body of water anywhere on the planet. The Arctic Ocean is almost enclosed by continents, but the Southern Ocean is its polar opposite in every sense, as it completely encircles an entire continent. The Southern Ocean supports enormous numbers of penguins, seals, and whales, all of which depend on it for their food. It is also a mighty engine room for the world's weather systems and it helps to drive the circulation of ocean currents, even those in the northern hemisphere. Storm-tossed and festooned with icebergs and extensive pack ice even in summer, the Southern Ocean is a formidable barrier for anyone trying to reach Antarctica. This becomes all-important for government agenices tasked with supporting human habitation there, because fuel and most supplies must be transported by sea. Consequently, the Southern Ocean has protected Antarctica from humans and has minimized our impact on the continent.

As the ancient supercontinent of Pangaea (250 million years ago) slowly broke up, the final piece to separate from the remaining continent of Gondwana was the bridge between the South American Andes and what is now the spine of the Antarctic Peninsula. Scientists are still debating exactly when this tumultuous tectonic event took place, though it is thought to be about 35 million years ago. As this gap opened up, however, it formed what we now know as the Drake Passage. The Southern Ocean was born. The Drake Passage gradually deepened and widened and as it did so the Antarctic Circumpolar Current formed. This belt of cold water continues to flow around Antarctica from west to east, effectively insulating the continent from the intrusion of warmer water from the north. As this superhighway of cold water strengthened, Antarctica started to rapidly cool down. The onset of glaciation led to the formation of an extensive icecap, with glaciers and ice shelves flowing seawards from a 15,750-ft (4,800-m) high dome of ice. In the Southern Ocean itself, the annual formation of sea ice became a regular and important feature.

An indication of the extent of the Southern Ocean is that it covers at least 15 percent of the total area of all the world's oceans, and it effectively isolates Antarctica. It is possible to sail around the coasts of all the world's other continents without crossing more than 62 miles (100 km) of open sea at any one time. However, Antarctica's nearest neighbor, South America, is 600 miles (1,000 km) away, across Drake Passage. The Southern Ocean extends as far north as the Antarctic Convergence Zone (also known as the Polar Front), which is a constantly changing biological boundary where the cold polar water meets and dives beneath the warmer waters from more temperate latitudes. The Convergence Zone is usually found between 45 and 59 degrees South and is characterized by fogs and a turbulent upwelling of ocean currents. The Convergence Zone also helps with a biological definition of what constitutes the boundary of Antarctica. Islands such as South Georgia and the South Sandwich group lie south of the Convergence in the Southern Ocean, and as such are considered part of Antarctica. Other island groups, such as Australia's Macquarie Island and New Zealand's Campbell Island, lie north of the Convergence, hence being thought of as subantarctic.

Although the Southern Ocean circulates from west to east there is also a current closer to the continent's coast that flows in the opposite direction, from east to west. This helps to create a turbulent mixing of waters. The upwelling of currents and nutrients also occurs around calving ice shelves and as large icebergs break up. Of even greater impact is the massive upwelling of deep cold water in the Southern Ocean close to the Antarctic Convergence. This mixing helps to oxygenate the water, making it biologically much richer than the less saline, highly stratified waters found in the Arctic. As oxygen dissolves in cold water much better than it does in warm, the chilly Southern Ocean is much more productive than tropical waters near the equator. Deep, cold Antarctic waters continue to flow all the way into northern hemisphere waters, influencing other ocean currents and climate.

The Southern Ocean

Compared to the Arctic, the Antarctic does not support many different species of mammals or birds, but the species that do live there occur in great numbers. The overall productivity of the Southern Ocean, though not as great as once thought, continues to have a major influence on the diversity and nature of the entire Antarctic ecosystem. In summer, when light levels are high and essential nutrients such as phosphates, nitrates, and silicates are brought to the surface, enormous quantities of plankton bloom to form the basis of the food chain. The myriad microscopic diatoms (unicellular algae) and phytoplankton produced are then consumed by zooplankton (copepods, amphipods etc) as well as the inch-long crustacean known as krill (*Euphausia superba*), perhaps the most abundant animal on Earth. Vast swarms of krill gradually form and move around the Southern Ocean depending on the shift of currents and plankton blooms (plankton are defined as all sea life that cannot swim faster than the ocean currents). In turn, krill are pursued and eaten by fish, seals, penguins, and other sea birds, with the filter-feeding baleen whales being at the top of the "krill pyramid." The abundance and distribution of krill swarms can be extremely patchy, so even a moderate change in temperature or current can create stress due to lack of food for the higher animals.

The formation of sea ice around Antarctica during winter months is one of the greatest natural events to occur annually on the planet. The freezing begins in late March and by the time it reaches its full extent in the early spring the area of sea ice effectively doubles the size of the continent. This helps to create a significant albedo effect (acting like a giant mirror to reflect the sun's rays), thereby influencing the world's weather systems, especially in the Southern Hemisphere. First-year sea ice is usually up to 6 ft (2 m) thick, but older ice can be as much as 16 ft (5 m). An epontic, red-brown algae commonly grows on the under surface of sea ice and is fed upon by krill.

Gravity-driven katabatic winds routinely funnel down onto the sea ice and the Southern Ocean from the high Polar Plateau, which in many places comes close to the coast. These powerful and extremely cold winds help to keep the coastal regions frigid. However, in places where there is also a strong upwelling of currents, the wind can help to keep a region free of ice throughout the winter.

148 HUMPBACK WHALES (MEGAPTERA NOVAEANGLIAE) SWIMMING NEAR THE MELCHOIR ISLANDS OFF THE COAST OF THE ANTARCTIC PENINSULA.

148-149 MAKING USE OF EVEN THE SMALLEST OF AIR CURRENTS, A BLACK-BROWED ALBATROSS (THALASSARCHE MELANOPHRYS) CAN GLIDE OVER THE SOUTHERN OCEAN FOR INCREDIBLE DISTANCES.

150-151 TABULAR ICEBERGS, HERE OFF THE PRINCE OLAV COAST, EAST ANTARCTICA, FORM WHEN THEY BREAK OFF ANTARCTICA'S ICE SHELVES AND GLACIER FRONTS. THEY GRADUALLY DRIFT NORTHWARDS BREAKING UP DUE TO WAVE ACTION AND MELTING.

152 TOP A DIVER PHOTOGRAPHS A GIANT MEDUSA'S BELL NEAR THE SURFACE OF THE SOUTHERN OCEAN. MEDUSAS CAN REACH OVER 3 FT (1 M) IN DIAMETER.

152-153 STARFISH ON THE SEA FLOOR OF THE SOUTHERN OCEAN FEED ON SEAL FAECES. A DIVER EXPLORES AN ICE CAVE BELOW A WEDDELL SEAL BREATHING HOLE.

153 A SUNSTAR FEEDS ON A PENGUIN CARCASS ABANDONED AFTER BEING KILLED BY A LEOPARD SEAL.

This is known as a polynya and though poorly understood it can provide vital resting and feeding places for birds and mammals.

There are 23,000 fish species in the world, but there are only some 120 known species in the Southern Ocean. These fish commonly have big bony heads and all have a glyco-protein in their circulation system to keep their blood (no red blood haemoglobin cells) from freezing, effectively acting like antifreeze in an automobile radiator. This is vital as the Southern Ocean remains at a constant 28.7°F (-1.8°C) all year. Remarkably, some of these fish species, such as the Antarctic cod (*Dissostichus mawsoni*), live at depths of 1,900 ft (600 m) and are a major food source for the deep-diving Weddell seal. The Antarctic sea floor is also covered in starfish, sponges, anemones, and various slow-growing benthic invertebrates.

Fishing fleets are now regular visitors to the Southern Ocean during the summer, with both national and un-flagged "pirate" vessels entering the lucrative market in recent years. This has sparked considerable debate about the effects of fishing, mainly because the growth patterns and population dynamics of these large bottom-dwelling fish remain poorly understood. So we still do not know if the catch is a fair and sustainable harvest or a tragedy. There is a significant squid fishery also operating in the Southern Ocean. Krill harvesting, once thought to be a massive source of protein for a hungry world, has stalled in recent years, largely due to the rapid denaturing of the protein after the krill is caught. What krill is taken from the Southern Ocean is processed straight away on board factory ships with much of it eventually being marketed as pet food and fertilizer.

Pelagic whaling still takes place in Southern Ocean waters, with the Japanese harpooning at least 300 minke whales each year. This has also sparked major debate and protest around the world for, given the horrific and sustained killing of whales throughout the first half of the 20th century, most recognize that the Southern Ocean's current designation as a whale sanctuary should remain sacrosanct.

In recent years there has been a proliferation of long-line fishing fleets operating in subantarctic and Southern Ocean waters. This has resulted in a major crash in the populations of many albatross species as the birds are attracted to the baited hooks on the 30-mile (50-km) long lines that are reeled out from the stern of ships. All too often, the birds are snared on the hooks and drown. Many also have their wings damaged by the line itself. Although clever systems are now in place to get the bait quickly below the surface before the diving albatrosses can catch it, many adult birds still die. Tragically, when one adult perishes it means that the surviving parent bird cannot bring back enough food for a growing chick, resulting in many more deaths back at the nesting sites.

The health of the Southern Ocean is paramount, both for its own sake as a wilderness and for its symbolic value as the guardian of Antarctica. As such, the proper management of the Southern Ocean is vital and the regulations of international agreements, such as the Convention for the Conservation of Antarctic Marine Living Resources and the Antarctic Treaty, must be enforced.

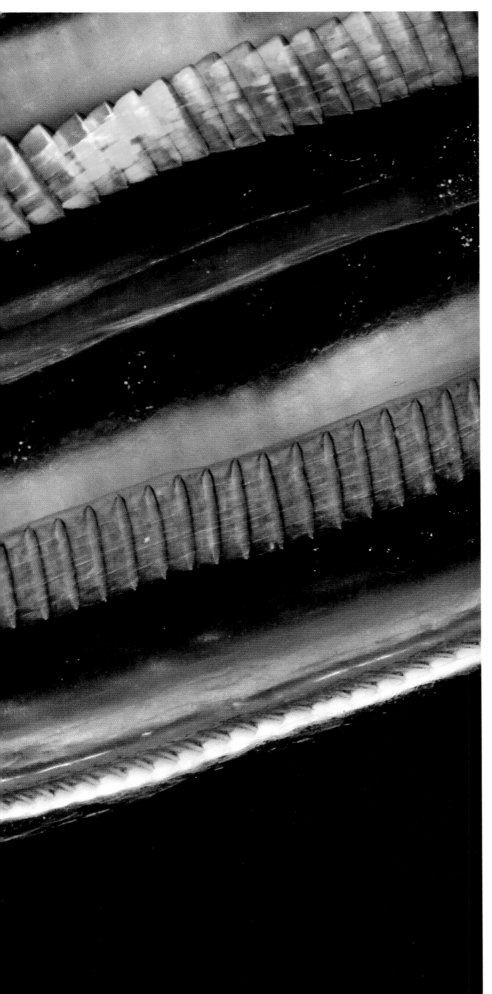

154-155 A CTENOPHORE OR COMB JELLY INGESTS AN ANTARCTIC KRILL.

155 TOP AN ANTARCTIC KRILL (EUPHAUSIA SUPERBA) WITH YELLOW ALGAE IN ITS STOMACH.

155 BOTTOM KRILL FEEDING; THIS SMALL SHRIMP-LIKE CRUSTACEAN IS THE MOST IMPORTANT ZOOPLANKTON IN THE ANTARCTIC MARINE FOOD CHAIN.

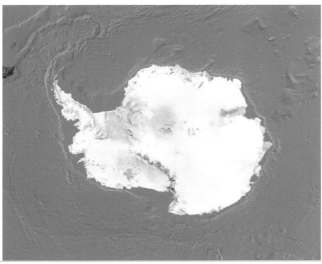

156 TOP AND 156-157 THE MOUNTAINOUS SPINE OF THE ANTARCTIC PENINSULA IS HEAVILY GLACIATED, WITH MANY GLACIERS FLOWING DOWN INTO THE SEA. ALTHOUGH HEAVILY GLACIATED, THE ANTARCTIC PENINSULA IS OFTEN CALLED THE "BANANA BELT" OF ANTARCTICA BECAUSE IT IS RELATIVELY WARM BY ANTARCTIC STANDARDS, WHICH MEANS THAT IT RECEIVES MORE SNOWFALL – UP TO SEVERAL FEET EACH YEAR. THERE IS ALSO MORE MELT AND DUE TO GLOBAL WARMING THE ANTARCTIC PENINSULA IS WARMING UP FASTER THAN ANYWHERE ELSE ON THE PLANET.

Glaciers and Ice Shelves

Images of Antarctica taken from space are dramatic and arrestingly beautiful. What stands out is the mother-of-pearl glow from the Polar Plateau – a rich lustrous core encircled by glistening sunlight reflected on a shattered jigsaw of ice floes, all set against a backdrop of the deep blue of the Southern Ocean. Other dominant features include the two massive, flat ice shelves that butt onto the continent. They are so vast that by comparison the ice sheets of the Arctic seem utterly trivial. On closer inspection of these incredible satellite images it ispossible to see the fractured surfaces of the glaciers. The awesome scale of these crevassed, moraine-flecked rivers of ice is simply breathtaking. This immense and unforgiving continent has been sculpted by natural forces that make all human endeavors seem insignificant. And yet it is human activity over the last century that has accelerated the rate of climate change to the point that it is having a detrimental influence on the glaciation of both polar regions.

The glaciation of Antarctica, which began some 35 million years ago with the break-up of the continent of Gondwanaland and the formation of the Antarctic Circumpolar Current, meant that the Polar Plateau started to take shape as the continent cooled down. What formed was a high, windswept frigid desert that now dominates the continent with an up to 15,700-m (4,800-m) thick covering of ice. Driven by the force of gravity and the almost plastic nature of the ice meant that it started flowing towards the sea. Ice either flows into the Southern Ocean as a glacier, or if it splays out into a large fan-shaped plain, it is known as an ice shelf. Antarctica has a multitude of major glaciers and ice tongues that poke out from the coast as well as two major ice shelves, the Filchner-Ronne and the Ross. There are also several smaller ice shelves, notably the Amery Ice Shelf, which has been created by the Lambert Glacier, the largest glacier on Earth.

In East Antarctica, the ice moves seawards in two major directions at once, pushing out across the Weddell Sea between the Antarctic Peninsula and the Coats Land coast, forming the Filchner-Ronne Ice Shelf. The smaller part of the ice shelf is called the Filchner after the German Wilhelm Filchner who, in 1911, tried to establish if the Weddell and Ross seas were connected by a land bridge or an ocean channel. The much larger section is called the Ronne, after Finn Ronne, an American expedition leader of the 1940s. The two shelves are separated by Berkner Island. In the other direction, however, the ice squeezes and "pours" through gaps in the Transantarctic Mountains. The famous Beardmore Glacier, which the Britsh explorers Shackleton and Scott both used to reach the Polar Plateau, is one such glacier that flows down to meet the Ross Sea. Here, all the Transantarctic glaciers are joined by yet more ice that is fed down from Marie Byrd Land on the West Antarctic Ice Sheet. As all this ice merges and spreads out across the surface of the sea, it forms the Ross Ice Shelf, the largest ice shelf in the world. Named for the British Captain James Clark Ross who discovered it in 1842, the Ross Ice Shelf soon became known as the Great Ross Barrier or simply the Barrier, for clearly it blocked all seaward progress to the south.

The Ross Ice Shelf is roughly the size of France and it varies in thickness between 2,300 ft (700 m) next to the Transantarctic Mountains and 1,000 ft (300 m) at its seaward edge – this is a huge chunk of ice. It is important to understand that the Ross Ice Shelf consists of freshwater glacier ice and is not sea ice, which is frozen salt water. Impressively, this seemingly vast, flat plain is actually floating and it flexes up and down twice each day with the tidal cycle. As pressure builds on the Ross Ice Shelf, it is relentlessly pushed from behind by the arrival of more ice. This stress, compounded by the impact of wave action at the seaward edge, results in large sections snapping off. These sections form the flat-topped, tabular icebergs so characteristic of the Southern Ocean, which can be so large and smooth that ski-equipped planes can land on them.

In 2000, a tabular iceberg labelled B-15 broke away from the Ross Ice Shelf and spent the next few years adrift in the Ross Sea.

It impacted on the distribution and build-up of sea ice and also affected both the movement of penguins trying to get to their colonies as well as the passage of ships in and out of Mc-Murdo Sound in the heart of the Ross Sea. B-15 was 183 miles (295 km) long and 23 miles (37 km) wide, with a surface area of 4,209 sq miles (10,915 sq km) and an estimated average thickness of 656 ft (200 m). B-15 gradually broke apart into smaller pieces (though still major icebergs in their own right), with each one taking years to drift northward and reaching as far as the tip of North Victoria Land.

Normally, an ice shelf is a balanced system where the inflow of ice roughly equals that lost through the calving of icebergs. Warmer temperatures, as have been experienced in Antarctica recently, can increase the flow rate of ice to such an extent that the result is a destabilization of the system, with the potential for a catastrophic collapse of the entire ice shelf. This collapse can be further accelerated by warm summer temperatures creating pools of surface melt-water that eventually leak down and weaken the base of the shelf. Crucially, if an ice shelf disintegrates, the glacier feeding it will accelerate even faster.

In 2002, satellite images captured the astounding break-up of the Larsen B Ice Shelf, which was attached to the eastern side of the Antarctic Peninsula. As the Larsen disintegrated, hundreds of huge tabular icebergs spewed into the Weddell Sea. Ominously, over the next 18 months, nearby glaciers started to flow eight times faster than normal. While the calving of icebergs or even the disintegration of the smaller ice shelves will not raise ocean levels in themselves, the resultant glacier acceleration certainly could. On both sides of the Antarctic Peninsula alone, where climate change has been most pronounced, no less than seven ice shelves and glacier systems have collapsed or partly disintegrated in recent years. That said, it is not envisaged that the two giant ones, the Filchner-Ronne and the Ross ice shelves, will entirely break-up in the near future. However, as more than 100 million people currently live within 3 ft (1 m) of sea level and the Antarctic continent holds enough ice to raise sea level by 187 ft (57 m), it does not take much imagination to envisage the catastrophic impact that the loss of these two ice shelves would have on low-lying islands and coastal communities around the world. In recent years, there have also been a large number of Arctic glaciers and small ice shelves collapsing across northern Canada and Greenland. It is has been postulated that due to climate change summer sea ice will be gone from the Arctic by 2050.

The collapse of Antarctic glaciers and sections of ice shelves over the last decade is unprecedented in recorded history. It is a clear warning beacon that global warming is very real. Indeed, as indicators of change, the ice shelves and glaciers of the polar regions have much to teach us about the health of the planet.

160 AND 161 AERIAL VIEWS OF A GLACIER IN WILHEMINA BAY
HIGHLIGHT THE MASSIVE CREVASSES THAT ARE FORMED AS THE
GLACIER FLOWS TO THE SEA.

162-163 THE BEARDMORE GLACIER IS ONE OF THE BIGGEST
GLACIERS TO FLOW THROUGH THE TRANSANTARCTIC
MOUNTAINS FROM THE POLAR PLATEAU DOWN TO THE ROSS
ICE SHELF. DISCOVERED IN 1909 BY BRITISH EXPLORER ERNEST
SHACKLETON, THE BEARDMORE BECAME THE ROUTE USED TO
GAIN ACCESS TO THE POLAR PLATEAU AND EVENTUALLY, BY
CAPTAIN SCOTT, THE SOUTH GEOGRAPHIC POLE.

Glacier and Ice Shelves

The Volcanoes of the Antarctic

The idea of volcanoes in Antarctica seems preposterous, somehow paradoxical, and yet they can be found near the Antarctic Peninsula, in the heart of the Ross Sea, and even on several groups of remote and widely dispersed subantarctic islands. Many of these hotspots are extremely active, with eruptions changing the shapes of beaches, destroying scientific bases, throwing volcanic bombs hundreds of feet into the air, and, recently, even pouring molten magma into the frigid Southern Ocean. Volcanoes also played a role in the Heroic Era of Antarctic exploration.

The volcanoes of the south polar regions are not only extraordinarily beautiful, but given their latitude and isolation they are also places of significant scientific interest. The international science community has long been puzzled by the geographic location of these volcanoes, their eruptive patterns, and the chemical composition of their gases. And yet Antarctica is seismically quiet with almost no recorded tectonic earthquakes. There are also volcanoes around the fringe of the Arctic, with volcanic activity in Alaska and the Aleutian Islands of North America, the Kamchatka Peninsula on the Pacific coast of Russia, and, perhaps the most famous and volatile of all, the thermal and geyser regions surrounding Iceland's volcanoes. However, despite their southern counterparts not being as well known or studied, the volcanoes of Antarctica have a fascination and a charm all their own. How amazing that there are smoking, ice-clad mountains surrounded by a stained-glass mosaic of sea ice, dotted with penguins and seals.

For most visitors to the Antarctic, the horseshoe-shaped Deception Island is their first contact with Antarctic volcanoes. Part of the South Shetland Islands, the low-lying Deception almost always attracts foul weather. Almost no matter how dismal the day appears at the outset, however, even a short visit to the island can create lasting impressions. Deception's contorted landscape is dramatic and moody, featuring hot, steaming ground enriched by a somber mosaic of red, ocher, black, and yellow

rocks. The island is surrounded by much bigger, heavily glaciated islands, such as Livingston, Smith, and King George. On a clear day the mountainous spine of the Antarctic Peninsula is visible across Bransfield Strait. Remarkably, a ship can sail through a narrow gap in Deception's cliffs known as Neptune's Bellows to emerge into Port Foster, which is in the center of the volcano's sunken caldera. In foggy conditions, Neptune's Bellows can be hard to find with distances from cliff edges near the entrance being quite deceptive. Therefore the name Deception was logically adopted in the 1820s by sealers and whalers. Today, after clearing the entrance and anchoring at Whaler's Bay in front of a derelict whaling station, wafts of steam and sulfurous gas that rise from vents beneath the black scoria beach are still immediately obvious to the eye and nose. In 1923, the water here became so acidic that it stripped the paint from the hulls of ships.

A major eruption in 1967 completely destroyed the Chilean science base Cerda at Pendulum Cove, located just above the beach at the far end of the caldera. It also badly damaged the British science base Biscoe House at Whaler's Bay, which had been established in the Second World War. Two years later, another powerful eruption forced the complete abandonment of the station and significantly altered the surrounding landscape.

Pendulum Cove remains a popular attraction, because, if the tide is right and the spirit brave, it is possible to bathe in a shallow, narrow strip of volcanically heated water beside the shore. It is also fascinating to climb up into the hills nearby to look down into a massive crater created during the 1960s eruptions. Only a few chinstrap penguins venture inside Deception's caldera with most found on the outer rim at the extensive Baily Head colony. Frequently, a few stray fur seals come ashore at the end of summer at Whaler's Bay to snooze amid the tangled wreckage of the whaling station. Above, on the lichen-draped cliffs near a gap in the rim known as Neptune's Window, a colony of cape or pintado (painted) petrels happily nests in the pockmarked crannies of the crumbly, ocher-colored rock.

164-165 THIS VOLCANIC CRATER LAKE FILLED WITH DARK GREEN WATER ON DECEPTION ISLAND WAS CREATED DURING ERUPTIONS IN THE 1960S. THE MAIN CALDERA BEHIND HAS ACCESS TO THE SEA.

165 TOP FUMEROLES UP TO 65 FT (20 M) HIGH POUR STEAM INTO THE -22° F (-30° C) AIR ON THE SUMMIT OF MT. EREBUS. THE DORMANT VOLCANO MT. DISCOVERY CAN BE SEEN IN THE DISTANCE.

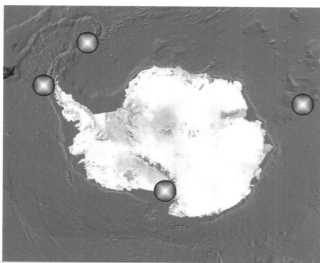

Leaving Deception and the South Shetlands behind and sailing 370 miles (600 km) northeast from the Antarctic Peninsula towards South Georgia, the first group of islands to be encountered is the South Orkneys. In 1903, a Scottish expedition came here in their ship *Scotia* and spent a year making scientific observations. Modern geologists studying Antarctic plate tectonics conferred the ship's name on the Scotia Arc, a 2,480-mile (4000-km) submarine ridge that divides the actively moving tectonic plates. The Scotia Arc stretches from the South Shetlands, through the Orkneys, then, after a spectacular loop, it curls back beneath the Southern Ocean to culminate in the high peaks of South Georgia. It then sweeps away westwards towards South America. At the Scotia Arc's eastern extremity lies the South Sandwich Islands, the wildest, most remote, and least visited of all Antarctic island groups.

First discovered by Captain James Cook in 1775 (with later significant discoveries in 1820 by the Russian, Thaddeus von Bellingshausen), the South Sandwich Islands consist of 11 islands spread along a 150-mile (240-km) long chain from 56 to 59 degrees South. They are formed by the rapid subduction of the South American tectonic plate beneath the tiny South Sandwich plate. (The South Sandwich plate is only eight million years old and is moving eastward at 3 inches [7 cm] per year.) The resultant temperature and pressure created by the rigid, colliding plates has altered the rocks and formed active basaltic volcanoes, such as Mt. Michael on Saunders Island. Other volcanoes are located on the rugged and partly glaciated islands of Thule, Bristol, Candlemas, and Zavodoski. In 2002, Montagu Island began an eruptive phase that grew in intensity over three years. Although rarely seen from ships and hard to observe even from space due to cloud cover, satellites in 2005 recorded that Montagu's highest peak, Mt. Belinda, was spewing molten lava spectacularly down its icy slopes. Fountaining like a giant waterfall, the lava cascaded into the Southern Ocean, creating large volumes of steam and, finally, new land. Eastward again from the South Sandwich Islands at 54 degrees South lies the dormant volcanic Bouvet Island, which is strictly in the subantarctic realm of the South Atlantic Ocean. Although discovered by the French as early as 1739, Bouvet was officially claimed by Norway in 1928, hence its proper Norwegian name of Bouvetoya. Bouvetoya is the remotest island in the world, with the nearest landmass, Dronning (Queen) Maud Land, East Antarctica, some 990 miles (1,600 km) away to the south.

166-167 CHINSTRAP PENGUINS (PYGOSCELIS ANTARCTICUS) CROWD ALONG THE BLACK VOLCANIC SCORIA BEACH AT BAILY HEAD ON THE OUTER RIM OF THE CALDERA OF THE ACTIVE VOLCANO ON DECEPTION ISLAND. THE CHINSTRAPS HAVE A LARGE BREEDING COLONY BEHIND THE GLACIER FRONT THAT IS STRIPED WITH LAYERS OF VOLCANIC ASH FROM ERUPTIONS IN 1967 AND 1969.

168-169 ADELIE (PYGOSCELIS ADELIAE) AND CHINSTRAP (PYGOSCELIS ANTARCTICUS) PENGUINS WADDLE ALONG A BLACK VOLCANIC BEACH ON SAUNDERS ISLAND, SOUTH SANDWICH ISLANDS.

170 TOP CHINSTRAP PENGUINS (PYGOSCELIS ANTARCTICUS) LEAP FROM A VOLCANIC ROCK CLIFF INTO SEETHING SURF.

170 BOTTOM AN AERIAL VIEW OF AN ACTIVE VOLCANO ON SAUNDERS ISLAND, SOUTH SANDWICH ISLANDS.

170-171 MILLIONS OF CHINSTRAP PENGUINS (PYGOSCELIS ANTARCTICUS) LIVE ON ZAVODOVSKI ISLAND, WHICH IS AN ACTIVE VOLCANO IN THE SOUTH SANDWICH ISLANDS. GREEN ALGAE STAINS THE SNOW.

The Volcanoes of the Antarctic

In the South Indian Ocean, at 49 degrees South, the volcano Mt. Ross on Grande Terre is the highest peak in the archipelago of 300 islands known as Isles Kerguelen. There have been no recorded eruptions on Mt Ross since the islands were discovered by the French in 1722, but active fumeroles still exist on its flanks. The "roaring forties" also host other island groups of volcanic origin, including the six French islands of Isles Crozet, at 46 degrees South, as well as South Africa's Marion Island in the Prince Edward Islands' group. These subantarctic islands all host breeding colonies of king, macaroni, rockhopper, and gentoo penguins. They are also home to many of the albatross and other seabird species.

By far the most beautiful volcano in all the subantarctic islands is Big Ben. Tucked away in the South Indian Ocean at 53 degrees South, the Big Ben massif is the heavily glaciated and dominant feature of Heard Island. At 9,006 ft (2,745 m), the summit of Big Ben, Mawson Peak, is the highest peak in Australia's territory. (The highest landmass in Australian Antarctic Territory is 12,470 ft/3,800 m above sea level and is a massive ice dome in East Antarctica, whereas the highest actual mountain on mainland Australia is Mt. Kosciusko, a mere 7,310 ft/2,228 m.) Big Ben has 12 glaciers originating from its 15.5-mile (25-km) wide summit caldera. The last known eruption was in 2001 when spectacular lava flows lit up the underside of clouds at night and were observed by the crew on an Australian government vessel. With fire and ice above and tussock grass and windswept beaches below, Heard Island is a precious wildlife reserve, choked with jostling king penguins and belching elephant seals – the Antarctic wilderness at its best.

The highest volcano on the continent of Antarctica is Mt. Sidley (13,717 ft/4,181 m) in Marie Byrd Land. However, there are also a number of others in this part of West Antarctica, such as Mt. Hampton, Mt. Takahe, and Mt. Steere, that are only slightly lower. Despite their massive bulk, all of these giants struggle to raise their summit calderas above the surrounding icecap. Perhaps Marie Byrd Land's most elegant volcano is Mt. Siple (10,203 ft/3,110 m). Its classic volcanic dome shape is best viewed from a ship cruising along the Siple Coast. There are other dormant volcanoes in Marie Byrd Land that do not raise their heads at all through the thick covering of the West Antarctic Ice Sheet.

At 11,138 ft (3,395 m), Mt. Overlord is the highest volcano in the section of the Transantarctic Mountains running through Victoria Land. Rocks on the summit have been dat-

ed to 7 million years and so it is considered extinct. Mt. Melbourne (8,963 ft/2,732 m), mid way down the Ross Sea coast of North Victoria Land, does exhibit volcanic activity, with steaming fumeroles and patches of warm soil near the summit. The highly adapted algae and microbes that grow in this niche, warm environment are carefully looked after under the Antarctic Treaty as this is designated a Specially Protected Area. Nearby, at Terra Nova Bay, there is an Italian scientific station. Mt. Melbourne is also famous because it has an emperor penguin colony located on the sea ice below.

In McMurdo Sound at 78 degrees South, there is a cluster of ancient volcanoes that includes Mt. Discovery, Mt. Morning and, on Ross Island itself, Terror and Terra Nova. The centerpiece of Ross Island is dominated by the 12,447 ft (3,794 m) high Mt. Erebus, Antarctica's most famous volcano. Unlike its much older, dormant neighbors, Erebus is in a constant state of activity, with a swirling and persistent lava lake (one of a very few anywhere in the world) and several times a day it erupts unpredictably, ejecting molten bombs high into the sky.

One hundred years ago, in March 1908, the first ascent of Mt. Erebus took place by a geological party from Ernest Shackleton's British Antarctic Expedition. Ever since this pioneering mixture of adventure and science, the volcano has held a fascination for both mountaineers and the scientific community. Since the mid-1970s, more detailed scientific work has been possible due to the better logistic support now available. Each summer dedicated teams work around the caldera, including geochemists who study the chemical composition of the gases that spew from the fumeroles at the summit. The seismic activity is also monitored remotely, with information transmitted from seismographs on the crater rim recorded 31 miles (50 km) away at New Zealand's Scott Base and at the U.S. McMurdo Station. While botanists have classified the highly specialized plants that thrive in the hot soil found around the summit.

Ever since 1842 when Sir James Clark Ross entered the Ross Sea on his ships *Erebus* and *Terror*, Antarctic volcanoes have presented a number of tough problems for scientists. Now, 166 years after Ross's voyage of discovery, we are starting to find answers for these geological puzzles. Whether they are located in the outer realm of the subantarctic or in the heart of the Ross Sea, Antarctic volcanoes will continue to capture our imagination. Antarctica remains an exquisitely beautiful yet mysterious land of ice and fire.

The Volcanoes of the Antarctic

174-175 *AN AERIAL VIEW OF MT. EREBUS WITH WIND CLOUDS OVER THE SUMMIT. THE BARNE GLACIER FLOWS DOWN OFF MT. EREBUS INTO MCMURDO SOUND.*

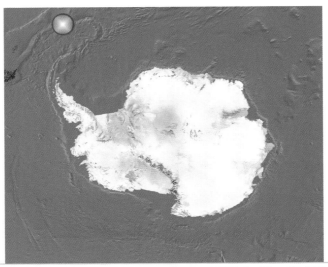

176 TOP AN AERIAL VIEW OF STROMNESS BAY. STROMNESS AND THE NEARBY LEITH AND HUSVIK BAYS EACH HAVE DERELICT NORWEGIAN WHALING STATIONS THAT DATE BACK TO THE EARLY 1900S.

176-177 THE ICE-CLAD SUMMIT OF MT. CUNNINGHAM RISES ABOVE SHALLOP COVE ON THE REMOTE SOUTHWEST COAST OF SOUTH GEORGIA.

177 BEAUTIFUL PEAKS LINE THE SPINE OF SOUTH GEORGIA AND THERE ARE NUMEROUS GLACIERS, MANY OF WHICH FLOW DOWN TO THE SEA.

South Georgia

South Georgia is the most beautiful island in the polar world; a stunning wildlife sanctuary of snow-covered peaks, emerald green bays, and deep blue glacier ice. It is an "oasis" on a storm-tossed Southern Ocean, the home for countless seals, penguins, and breeding seabirds, including the mighty albatrosses. There are also herds of reindeer which were introduced by Norwegian whalers. Although South Georgia has the characteristics of a subantarctic island it is truly part of Antarctica, as it lies south of the Antarctic Convergence Zone where cold Southern Ocean water flows beneath warmer mid-latitude seas. Sir Ernest Shackleton called the island "The gateway to Antarctica." Isolated in the South Atlantic Ocean, South Georgia's brooding, heavily glaciated mountains are often shrouded by storm clouds. Wind-blown, ice-cold mists lacerate the island's steep, fissured glaciers, their icefalls tumbling seawards into bays and fjords, choking them with icebergs and ice. And always on South Georgia there is the wind. An unpredictable hurricane-force, mind-numbing wind that pounds the coastline. The wind can be of such ferocity that it will disorient or blow you over with ease, destroy campsites, and, when anchors drag, ground ships. Then, inexplicably, there is utter calm. Perfect peace. For mountaineers, mariners, scientists, and tourists, South Georgia commands the utmost respect. Rising abruptly from the Southern Ocean, South Georgia has a raw wildness and sense of remoteness far greater than anywhere in the Arctic, even the archipelago of Svalbard or vast Greenland. You cannot buy an air ticket to South Georgia, or expect rescue. Those who sail towards the island do so with great excitement, trepidation, a deep sense of history, and a longing to get close to wildlife that has no fear of humans. Around its coasts, South Georgia heaves with the most endearing, quixotic collection of wildlife imaginable. It is an incomparable experience to stand on a beach in front of a colony of trumpeting, jostling king penguins and their fluffy brown chicks. That is, if you can get ashore through the surging surf onto beaches guarded by fur seals and foul-mouthed elephant seals that lumber over the pebbles, crushing anything in their path. Overhead, sooty albatrosses are often heard crying their haunting "peeee-aaah" as they soar over clifftops in perfect synchronized flight. This is also the home of the greatest long-distance flier of them all, the wandering albatross. To sit quietly alongside the wildlife of South Georgia is one of life's great privileges.

178-179 *AFTER SPENDING THE WINTER AT SEA A BULL ELEPHANT SEAL (*MIROUNGA LEONINA) *CRASHES THROUGH THE SURF ON TO A SOUTH GEORGIA BEACH.*

South Georgia

South Georgia

South Georgia

South Georgia's closest neighbor is the Falkland Islands 870 miles (1,400 km) away to the west, with the Antarctic continent some 930 miles (1,500 km) to the south across the storm-tossed Southern Ocean. A crescent-shaped island, some 105 miles (170 km) long by 18 miles (30 km) wide, South Georgia is studded with elegant alpine peaks. Mt. Paget (9,625 ft/2,934 m) is the highest peak and the dominant feature of the impressive Allardyce Range. There are 12 other peaks exceeding 6,500 ft (2,000 m), including some in the alluring Salvesen Range. Along with the nearby South Orkney Islands and the active volcanoes of the South Sandwich islands, South Georgia is part of the Scotia Arc, which is a submarine ridge that extends in a gigantic north-easterly sweep away from the Antarctic Peninsula.

Although South Georgia was sighted as early as 1675 it was Captain James Cook who first stepped ashore in 1775 to claim and name the island for King George III. Cook was disappointed when he realized that he had discovered an island instead of the hoped-for tip of the great southern continent. It was Cook's reports, however, that resulted in British and American sealers setting sail for South Georgia and the South Shetland Islands off the tip of the Antarctic Peninsula. In only 40 years from 1788 they plundered the fur seal population to near extinction, with at least one million hides being taken. Today, the fur seal numbers have bounced back to some 2.5 million, which may even be a greater number than there were originally. Many beaches are almost impossible to land on as fur seals will vigorously defend their territory. As pressure grows on breeding sites the seals climb high above the beaches, causing considerable damage to the tussock grass vegetation. It is a great joy to sit quietly on a South Georgia beach and watch dozens of fur seal pups as they cavort and play with each other on kelp-laden rocks.

184 AND 185 TOP WONDERFUL
MOUNTAINS RISE ABOVE ST. ANDREWS BAY
ON THE NORTH COAST OF SOUTH
GEORGIA. ST. ANDREWS IS FAMOUS FOR ITS
LARGE KING PENGUIN (APTENODYTES
PATAGONICUS) COLONY.

184-185 DAWN LIGHTS UP MT. SUGARTOP
(7,627 FT/2,325 M) NEAR GRYTVIKEN.
INCREASINGLY, EXPERIENCED YACHT
CREWS ARE CHARTERED BY
MOUNTAINEERING EXPEDITIONS TO LAND
THEM AT THE BASE OF SOUTH GEORGIA'S
PEAKS, MANY OF WHICH REMAIN
UNCLIMBED.

186 TOP GRYTVIKEN WHALING STATION IS NOW BEING DISMANTLED, WITH PRECAUTIONS BEING TAKEN TO AVOID ANY POLLUTION FROM ITS OIL AND ASBESTOS. A SUPERB MUSEUM HAS BEEN SET UP BY THE BRITISH WHO ALSO MAINTAIN A SCIENTIFIC STATION (SEEN AT LOWER LEFT) CALLED KING EDWARD POINT.

South Georgia

It is, however, the hunting of whales in the seas around South Georgia from 1904 to 1965 that really put the island on the map. In the early 1900s six major Norwegian shore-based whaling stations were established in the sheltered, glacier-free bays along the north coast. Incredible numbers of blue and other large whales were killed and processed during this period. The valuable whale oil was highly sought after for lamps, lubrication, and foodstuffs, such as margarine. In 1925 alone some 5,700 fin and 3,700 blue whales were slaughtered. Today, only the Japanese continue whaling for a relatively limited number of minke whales in the deep Southern Ocean and the whaling bases on South Georgia lie abandoned and rusting. Installations such as Grytviken have now largely been dismantled and their asbestos and waste oil buried or removed. There is now an exquisite museum at Grytviken that documents not only the rich diversity of South Georgia's flora and fauna, but also the island's history of exploration, whaling, mountaineering, and scientific research.

South Georgia will forever be linked to the British Antarctic explorer Sir Ernest Shackleton. His Trans-Antarctic expedition ship *Endurance* sank in the Weddell Sea in 1916, and the story of the crew's survival and Shackleton's voyage in a lifeboat to South Georgia and crossing of that island to initiate a rescue remains one of the great epics of Antarctic exploration. In 1922, Shackleton died at Grytviken and is buried in the whaler's cemetery. Today, South Georgia attracts many seaborne visitors keen to observe the wildlife, to climb the peaks or simply to pay homage to Shackleton who crossed the heart of the island on his route from King Haakon Bay to Stromness whaling station.

In 1982, the British Antarctic Survey's scientific base at King Edward Point (close to Grytviken) was severely disrupted when an Argentine military force invaded South Georgia, sparking the short but bloody Falklands War, which was fought largely on the Falkland Islands. South Georgia has the unfortunate distinction of being the only part of Antarctica to have been directly involved in a war. Today, South Georgia is administered by the South Georgia and South Sandwich Government based in Port Stanley the capital of the Falkland Islands.

186-187 WITH THE SUMMITS OF THE ALLARDYCE RANGE GLISTENING ON THE HORIZON, A RECENT SNOWFALL BLANKETS THE OLD NORWEGIAN WHALING STATION OF GRYTVIKEN.

187 TOP AN ANTARCTIC FUR SEAL (ARCTOCEPHALUS GAZELLA) SITS ATOP RUSTING OIL BARRELS AT ONE OF THE OLD WHALING STATIONS.

187 BOTTOM NOW THAT THE WHALING ERA IS OVER, A WHALE CHASER LIES ABANDONED AND STRANDED ON THE BEACH AT GRYTVIKEN.

188 AND 189 THE NORTHEAST COAST OF SOUTH GEORGIA IS FAMOUS FOR ITS LARGE KING PENGUIN (APTENODYTES PATAGONICUS) COLONIES, SUCH AS THOSE AT ST. ANDREWS, SALISBURY PLAIN, ROYAL BAY, AND RIGHT WHALE BAY. THE KING PENGUIN WITH ITS STUNNINGLY BEAUTIFUL PLUMAGE IS SLIGHTLY SMALLER THAN THE EMPEROR, AND ITS ANTICS CAN BE COMICAL.

190-191 A JOSTLING CROWD OF KING PENGUINS FILL THE COLONY AT GOLD HARBOUR. MALE AND FEMALE KING PENGUINS HAVE IDENTICAL PLUMAGE AND SO ARE ALMOST IMPOSSIBLE TO TELL APART. KINGS HAVE AN UNUSUAL 18-MONTH BREEDING CYCLE, WHICH MEANS THAT THERE ARE ALMOST ALWAYS CHICKS PRESENT IN THE COLONIES.

South Georgia

The combination of South Georgia's alpine landscape with its prolific wildlife is hard to beat. Any one of the massive king penguin colonies at the Bay of Isles (40,000 pairs), St. Andrews Bay (39,000 pairs), or Royal Bay (9,000 pairs) will have a huge emotional and visual impact on any visitor. As the king penguin has a unique 18-month breeding cycle there are always fat "oakum boy" chicks (as the sealers called them) huddled in the colonies waiting to harass the adult birds when they return from the sea with fish or krill. King penguin colonies can be extremely noisy and muddy places, so it is wonderful to see clusters of adult birds coming down to the beach to escape their chicks and to wash and preen their feathers in the surf. The king penguin is slightly smaller and lighter than its famous cousin the emperor from the heartland of Antarctica, however, the king's orange and yellow neck plumage is by far the most vibrant and striking of all the 16 penguin species.

South Georgia

192 A KING PENGUIN PARENT REGURGITATES A SLURRY OF SQUID AND KRILL INTO ITS CONSTANTLY HUNGRY CHICK'S MOUTH.

192-193 BROWN, DOWN-COVERED KING PENGUIN CHICKS HUDDLE TOGETHER IN THE COLONY AT RIGHT WHALE BAY.

193 TOP A TUBBY BARREL-SHAPED KING PENGUIN CHICK ("OAKUM BOY") TRIPS OVER TO LAND IN THE SNOW AT RIGHT WHALE BAY.

194-195 SOUTH GEORGIA IS FAMOUS FOR STRONG WINDS, SO IT IS COMMON FOR BLIZZARDS OF SNOW TO ALMOST COVER THE KING PENGUINS AT ST. ANDREWS BAY.

There are also chinstrap, gentoo, and macaroni penguin colonies dotted about South Georgia, though they often breed on steeper, tussock-covered ground, sometimes even on cliff edges. The macaroni is the most numerous penguin in the world (nine million) and they are found on most of the circumpolar subantarctic islands, with those on South Georgia forming perhaps the largest breeding colonies of this species. The macaroni is heavier and taller than the rockhopper, which is more commonly associated with the Falklands, and its bushy yellow eyebrow plumes of feathers give it a comical appearance in tune with its name, which originates from the folk song "Yankee Doodle."

South Georgia

The penguins may be the endearing clowns of South Georgia, but there are many other seabird species, such as petrels, shags, skuas, terns, and pintail ducks. However, it is the graceful albatrosses that stand out as the real stars of the show. Serene, slightly aloof, and each with stunning plumage, the black-browed, gray-headed sooty albatrosses are graceful and powerful fliers, even in the toughest of conditions.

The wandering albatross holds pride of place both for its size — wingspan 8–11 ft (2.5–3.5 m), weight 13–24 pounds (6–11 kg) — and in the huge distances it covers across the Southern Ocean in search of squid, its principal food. Wandering albatrosses have been recorded on several occasions circumnavigating the globe in the southern latitudes, with one covering 15,500 miles (25,000 km) in 9 weeks. Their ability to navigate over a vast ocean to find tiny dots of land, such as South Georgia, is still improperly understood and extraordinarily impressive (it probably involves the sun, stars, and magnetic force lines).

All albatross species are now threatened as significant numbers are drowning as a bycatch from long-line fishing techniques.

Tragically, if one adult dies then the other parent cannot bring back enough food to the nest to keep the fledgling alive.

All South Georgia bird and animal species are totally protected. Local fishing operations are also closely monitored so as to minimize the impact on albatross populations and to ensure that overfishing does not happen. South Georgia's management plan for future scientific research projects, fishing, and tourism is finely tuned and strictly implemented to ensure that this precious island remains so spectacularly beautiful and unspoilt.

198 TOP A JUVENILE WANDERING ALBATROSS (DIOMEDEA EXULANS) STRETCHES ITS WINGS ON THE TUSSOCK PRION ISLAND THAT LIES OFF THE NORTH COAST OF SOUTH GEORGIA.

198 BOTTOM AN AGGRESSIVE PREDATOR OF PENGUIN CHICKS, ANTARCTIC SKUAS (CATHARACTA ANTARCTICA) OFTEN SQUABBLE AMONG THEMSELVES, FIGHTING OVER PENGUIN EGGS, CHICKS, AND THE AFTERBIRTH OF SEALS.

199 THE DARK-MANTLED SOOTY ALBATROSS (PHOEBETRIA FUSCA) NESTS IN COLONIES AND LAYS A SINGLE EGG IN A LARGE NEST. THE PHOTOGRAPH WAS TAKEN ON PRION ISLAND, SOUTH GEORGIA.

200-201 LENTICULAR CLOUDS FORMING OVER A SOUTH GEORGIA HEADLAND INDICATE THAT THERE ARE POWERFUL WINDS BLOWING ACROSS THE TOP OF THE ISLAND'S PEAKS.

The Falkland Islands

It may seem strange to include the Falkland Islands in a book about Antarctica, especially as these self-governing British islands are inhabited by sheep farmers, 500,000 sheep, fishermen, and military personnel. The capital city, Stanley, has a a cathedral and a population of 2,000, which is two-thirds of the total population. The rest of the Falklanders live in smaller settlements or in the countryside known as the "camp." In 1982, the Falklands were the focus of world attention due to a bitter, two month-long war between Argentina and Great Britain. The war also impacted heavily on South Georgia, a principal gateway to Antarctica. Argentina was defeated in its attempt to claim the Islas Malvinas, their name for the Falklands, and the local residents remain staunchly British. However, located in the extreme South Atlantic Ocean, this beautiful archipelago is in essence about as subantarctic as any of the other islands around the rim of the Southern Ocean. At 51 degrees South, the Falklands are roughly at the same latitude as Bouvetoya, Heard Island, and the Auckland Islands. Certainly, the Falklands have thriving colonies of magellanic, gentoo, and rockhopper penguins, and even a small colony of breeding king penguins, as well as other seabirds such as the black-browed albatross. The Falklands are a wildlife paradise par excellence. Because the islands lie in the path of ships heading for Cape Horn, there are various reports of sightings of the islands from 1660 to the early 1700s by Dutch, Spanish, and French navigators. However, the earliest sighting is thought to be a British ship in 1592. The Falklands' rugged coastline is littered with shipwrecks from the days of sail. There is also evidence of earlier visits by humans arriving by dug-out canoe possibly from Tierra del Fuego. Evidence of the fox-like dog known as a warrah (now extinct) has also been found. It is also possible that the first human settlers came via a land bridge during the last ice age.

The Falklands lie on the edge of the relatively shallow Patagonian continental shelf and are divided into two main islands, West Falkland and East Falkland, with some 700 other smaller, outlying islands, and a total land area of 4,600 sq miles (12,000 sq km). The highest peak on East Falkland is Mt. Usborne, which rises 2,312 ft (705 m) above a bog plain. Argentina's Patagonian coast lies 300 miles (482 km) away to the west, while 690 miles (1,110 km) across open ocean to the east lies South Georgia. Unlike the other subantarctic islands, it is possible to fly to the Falklands from both the UK and Chile. The British Antarctic Survey (BAS: once called the Falkland Islands Dependencies Survey) fly support aircraft from Stanley's airport along the spine of the Antarctic Peninsula to land at the BAS base Rothera, on Adelaide Island. The Falkland Islands are unquestionably an important access route to Antarctica.

The Falklands are rightly known as one of the great destinations to view certain species of penguin and other seabirds. With the sheep industry in decline, there has been a corresponding increase in both fishing and hydrocarbon exploration around the islands. Ecotourism, however, is also a rapidly expanding business. Many ornithologists, photographers, and painters now come to the Falklands as part of a farm-stay and guided wildlife experience, or as part of a seaborne package that includes the Antarctic Peninsula and South Georgia. As many of the islands, such as Saunders, Sea Lion, and New islands, are privately owned, farmers have become ardent conservationists and very protective of the creatures that live and breed on the edges of their property. Strict environmental regulations are in place.

There are a variety of habitats for plants and birds in the Falklands, from open sand dunes to the marshy higher ground with moist, peaty bogs. Peat is still dug and burned for home heating. Close to the coast there are thick bands of six-feet high tussock grass (*Parodiochloa flabellate*), which can reach 9–13 ft (3–4 m) high where it is not over-grazed by sheep. The base of the tussock pedestals provide perfect sites for nesting burrows for many bird species, such as magellanic penguins, prions, shearwaters, and petrels. Other species, such as the passerines (wrens, siskins, and thrushes), birds of prey (striated caracara, turkey vulture, and short-eared owl), and coastal seabirds (kelp geese and flightless steamer duck), also rely on the tussock for shelter, especially during the numerous batterings by the prevailing westerly winds. Quite a few cetacean species live in the seas around the islands, with several dolphin species, such as the Commerson's (*Cephalorhynchus commersonii*) and the Peale's (*Lagenorhynchus australis*), often found playing in the inshore channels.

202-203 THE PRIVATELY OWNED BEAVER ISLAND WITH ITS RUGGED HEADLANDS AND STORM-SWEPT BEACHES IS TYPICAL OF THE GROUP OF ISLANDS THAT MAKE UP THE FALKLANDS.

203 TOP THE FALKLAND ISLANDS LIE BETWEEN THE SOUTH ATLANTIC AND THE SOUTHERN OCEAN AND SO ARE FREQUENTLY LASHED BY STRONG WINDS AND BIG WAVES.

204-205 GENTOO PENGUINS (PYGOSCELIS PAPUA) FACE STORMY CONDITIONS ON A FALKLANDS BEACH.

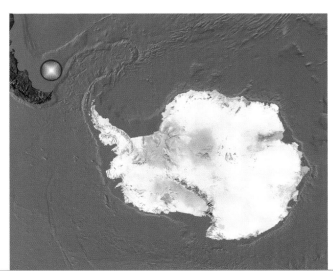

The Falkland
Islands

206 AND 206-207 GENTOO PENGUINS JUMPING THROUGH
KELP BEDS AND SURF TO COME ASHORE TO THEIR BREEDING
COLONY. GENTOO PENGUINS ARE EASILY IDENTIFIED BY THEIR
DISTINCTIVE ORANGE BEAKS AND LITTLE WHITE CAP OF
FEATHERS. THEY ARE COMMON ON THE FALKLAND ISLANDS
AND ALSO BREED ON SOUTH GEORGIA AND THE WESTERN
EDGE OF THE ANTARCTIC PENINSULA.

The Falkland
Islands

208 AND 208-209 GENTOO PENGUINS (PYGOSCELIS PAPUA)
SURFING ASHORE IN THE FALKLAND ISLANDS. SURF COMMONLY
POUNDS THE YELLOW SAND BEACHES OF THE FALKLANDS,
SO GENTOO PENGUINS HAVE BECOME VERY EXPERIENCED
AT CRASHING THROUGH THE WAVES TO REACH THEIR
BREEDING COLONY. PENGUINS HAVE STRONG BREAST BONES
THAT PROTECT THEM WHEN DEALING WITH THE SURF
OR ROCKY SHORES.

210 STRIATED CARACARAS, OR JOHNNY ROOKS,
(PHALCOBOENUS AUSTRALIS) HANG AROUND THE EDGE
OF ALBATROSS AND PENGUIN COLONIES WAITING TO PREY
ON WEAK CHICKS.

210-211 A COLONY OF BLUE-EYED SHAGS (PHALACROCORAX
ATRICEPS) OCCUPY A ROCKY HEADLAND ABOVE A TYPICAL
FALKLAND ISLANDS BEACH.

The Falkland Islands

212-213 AN ADULT ROCKHOPPER PENGUIN (EUDYPTES CHRYSOCOME) AT CAPE BOUGAINVILLE ON EAST FALKLAND, FALKLAND ISLANDS. THESE PENGUINS LIVE IN COLONIES ON STEEP, GRASSY SLOPES, WHICH THEY OFTEN SHARES WITH ALBATROSSES AND CORMORANTS.

Off the coast, the hourglass dolphin (*Lagenorhynchus cruciger*), long-finned pilot whales (*Globicephela melas*), orca (*Orincus orca*), and sperm whales (*Physeter macrocephalus*) are reasonably common too.

Elephant seals, those great, ocean-going sea mammals, love to haul out on the beach to create wallows in the mud or among the tussocky sand dunes. Often, during the warm summer months, they just snooze in groups on the pristine beaches, casually flipping sand over the moulting skin on their backs to keep themselves cool. A gaggle of glistening upland geese wander disdainfully past the seals, seemingly unconcerned about the massive size and weight difference between them. Then a line of black and white-striped magellanic penguins straggle by, corkscrewing and raising their necks as they draw level with the seals, to bray loudly in their ears like a donkey. In fact, the magellanic penguin is commonly called the jackass.

More wary and aloof of both humans and other animals, the South American sea lions also inhabit these remote

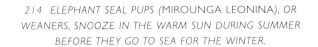

beaches as well as the kelp-strewn rock ledges beneath the cliffs. The big male sea lions are quite aggressive, especially when protecting their harem of females who are suckling their cute, plump pups. It is a wonderful spectacle of power and agility to watch a sea lion hunting a rockhopper penguin in the water as it tries to land through the surf onto a rock ledge. Relying on numbers and speed, wave after wave of rockhoppers crash ashore through the kelp, each one flapping its flippers madly to scrabble up the rock and evade capture from the sea lion's snapping jaws. The majority make it and then begin an arduous climb to the colony up the cliff face, leaping from ledge to ledge to reach their ravenous chicks.

Remarkably, the rockhopper penguin breeding colony is perfectly integrated alongside the nesting sites of thousands of black-browed albatrosses. The nests are sited at just the right distance apart so as not to create total mayhem as the animals come and go from feeding their offspring. The blackbrows construct a 12-inch (30-cm) high pedestal of mud and grass that is dish-shaped so that the heat is held in around the egg when the parent bird squats on top. The rockhoppers nest is lower, made of mud, feathers, and grass, or sometimes little more than a few hurriedly gathered stones. Unlike the albatross, the rockhopper commonly has two chicks. Despite the daily climb up and down the cliff to reach their feeding grounds at sea, it is worthwhile for the rockhoppers to nest on cliff tops as their nests are located on well-drained sites and safe from large waves. For the majestic albatross, of course, wind is essential for flight and maneuvering, so the clifftop is the logical place to stretch its long wings and the strong winds aid its take-off.

As the animals of the Falklands have not been hunted mercilessly, there remains an important level of trust that humans are not predators to be feared. As with Antarctica, the Falklands are still a place where it is privilege to sit quietly on a beach and have a parade of penguins walk right past you, completely unconcerned by your presence. This sense of fellowship is precious and must be maintained at all costs.

214 ELEPHANT SEAL PUPS (MIROUNGA LEONINA), OR WEANERS, SNOOZE IN THE WARM SUN DURING SUMMER BEFORE THEY GO TO SEA FOR THE WINTER.

214-215 AN ELEPHANT SEAL MALE ON SEA LION ISLAND LIES IN A WALLOW OF OTHER SEALS WHILE HIS SKIN MOULTS DURING THE SUMMER.

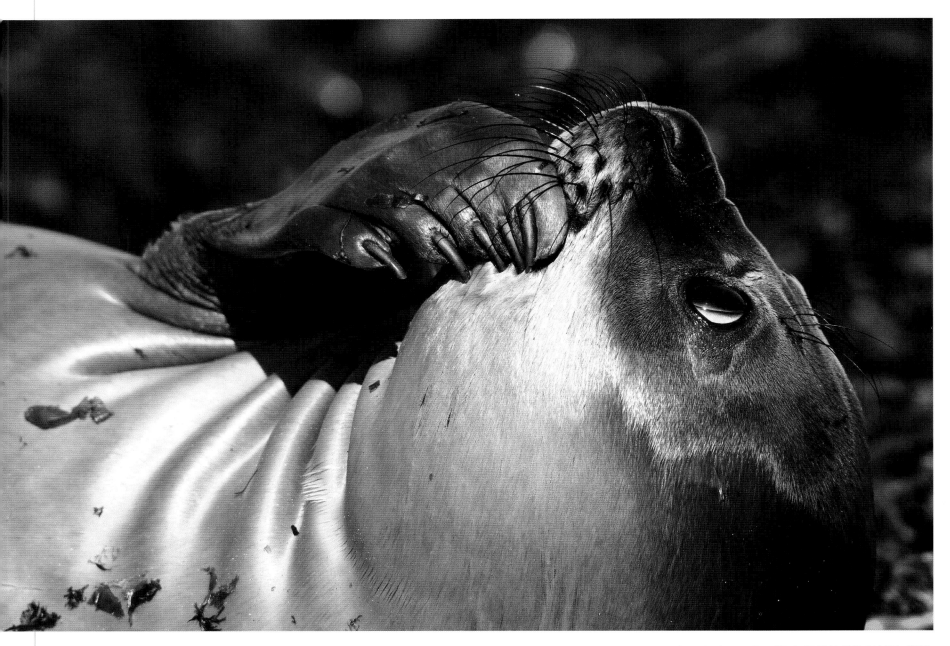

216 AND 217 A YAWNING ELEPHANT SEAL PUP ON SEA LION ISLAND. ELEPHANT SEAL PUPS GROW VERY QUICKLY BECAUSE THEIR MOTHER'S MILK IS EXTREMELY FAT-RICH. BY THE END OF THE SUMMER THEY WILL BE STRONG ENOUGH TO GO TO SEA FOR THE WINTER AND THEY WILL NOT COME ASHORE AGAIN UNTIL THE FOLLOWING SPRING.

218-219 MAGELLANIC PENGUINS (SPHENISCUS MAGELLANICUS) COME ASHORE TO OCCUPY THEIR NESTS, WHICH ARE DEEP BURROWS IN THE SAND BENEATH TUSSOCK GRASS. THESE PENGUINS HAVE A DISTINCTIVE BRAYING SOUND LIKE A DONKEY.

220 AND 220-221 BLACK-BROWED ALBATROSSES (THALASSRACHE MELANOPHRIS) RETURN FROM THE SOUTHERN OCEAN WITH SQUID TO FEED THEIR CHICKS WHO OCCUPY NESTS MADE OF MUD AND GRASS.

The Falkland Islands

222 AND 223 THERE ARE NUMEROUS COLONIES OF
BLACK-BROWED ALBATROSSES THROUGHOUT THE FALKLANDS.
THESE BIRDS FLY HUGE DISTANCES OVER THE SOUTHERN
OCEAN IN SEARCH OF SQUID. HOWEVER, MANY HAVE BEEN
KILLED AS A BY-CATCH IN THE EXPANDING FISHING INDUSTRY
AROUND THE FALKLANDS.

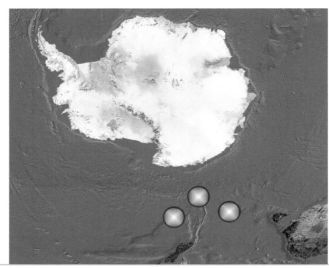

*224 TOP MEGAHERBS
(PLEUROPHYLLUM SPECIOSUN) IN
FLOWER ON A WIND-BLOWN COAST IN
THE SOUTHWEST OF CAMPBELL ISLAND.

224-225 COMPLEX GEOLOGIC LAYERING
ON THE STORM-LASHED WESTERN COAST
OF THE COL-AZIMUTH SADDLE,
CAMPBELL ISLAND. THANKS TO A
DETERMINED EFFORT BY THE NEW
ZEALAND GOVERNMENT, IN RECENT
YEARS MOST OF THEIR SUBANTARCTIC
ISLANDS ARE NOW TOTALLY FREE OF
RATS, SO REDUCING THE IMPACT ON
NESTING SEABIRD CHICKS. THERE ARE
STILL WILD PIGS ON CAMPBELL ISLAND.*

ANTARCTICA - ANTARCTICA - ANTARCTICA - ANTARCTIC

The New Zealand Subantarctic Islands

Isolated, rugged, windswept, and breathtakingly beautiful, the five groups of subantarctic islands that lie just south of New Zealand are all fragile ecosystems that are now strictly protected. These islands are home to many animal and plant species that are endemic, that is, they exist only here on the fringe of the storm-tossed Southern Ocean. Unlike many other subantarctic islands, the New Zealand islands have no permanent snow cover or glaciers.

All five island groups – the Snares Islands, Auckland Islands, Antipodes Islands, Bounty Islands, and Campbell Island – were recognized in 1998 as worthy of World Heritage status. New Zealand's Department of Conservation (DoC) is now charged with protecting and preserving these islands in perpetuity. They are also classified as national nature reserves, which is New Zealand's highest classification. All visitors, be they scientist or tourist, must be accompanied by a DoC representative and, operating under a closely supervised permit, abide by a strict minimum impact code. This chain of islands is closely linked to the entire southwest coast (Te Wahipounamu) of New Zealand's South Island, which is also designated as a World Heritage Site. The nearest neighbor to the west is Australia's Macquarie Island, also a World Heritage subantarctic island. The United Nations Environment Program described the New Zealand subantarctic islands as "the most diverse and extensive of all subantarctic archipelagos."

The northernmost of the five island groups is the Snares, which lies in the "Roaring Forties" at 47 degrees South, some 62 miles (100 km) southwest of Stewart Island (Rakiura), the smallest of New Zealand's three main islands. The southernmost and perhaps the most well known due to its long-serving (though now closed) year-round scientific base is Campbell Island, at 52 degrees South. Cool-temperate, wet, and windy, Campbell lies firmly in the "Furious Fifties" and is battered by the wildest weather the Southern Ocean has to offer.

All the islands are now uninhabited, however, there have been ill-fated attempts at farming and Maori settlements, as well as once being regular haunts for the rapacious sealers and whalers. As early as 1842, James Clark Ross called in here after his remarkable discoveries further south in the Antarctic. Over the past 200 years, the rugged coastlines have claimed a fair number of ships and there are some extraordinary tales of survival by the stranded crews. One shipwrecked seaman in 1864 described his subantarctic refuge as plagued by "incessant gales, constant hail, snow and pelting rain," much worse in his experience than anything found elsewhere in the Southern Ocean, even near the feared Cape Horn. The islands were once stocked with emergency castaway food, but they are now about as pristine as it is possible to make them. All the wild sheep, goats, rabbits, and cattle have been systematically removed. In recent years, the DoC has also completed the formidable task of eliminating all the pests, such as the rats and cats, which had the potential to decimate the populations of burrowing seabirds. The New Zealand subantarctic region is renowned for its great concentration of seabirds, with at least 40 species breeding there. The islands lie just north of the Antarctic Convergence, which is a biologically productive zone where the upwelling of deep, nutrient-rich water from the cold Southern Ocean mixes with the shallow, warmer waters of the Campbell Plateau. This means that the seas around the islands are rich in food. Seabirds use their island homes as bases from which to forage out at sea for krill and squid to bring back to their chicks.

Pelagic fin-fish and squid also exist in great numbers in these waters, thereby supporting a lucrative fishing industry that is now closely monitored by New Zealand patrol vessels and aircraft. New Zealand's Exclusive Economic Zone extends for some 230 miles (370 km) around the islands and is one of the most extensive anywhere in the world. Over the last decade or so, however, the tragic by-catch of albatrosses and sea lions in long-lines or trawling nets has been a deeply troubling and controversial issue. Some albatross populations have crashed spectacularly. In 2003, in an attempt at added protection, a marine reserve was declared, providing a safe haven for all life up to 14 miles (22 km) offshore from each coastline.

226 ROCKHOPPER PENGUINS (EUDYPTES CHRYSOCOME)
ON BOULDERS AT THE BASE OF A WATERFALL AT
SMOOTHWATER BAY, CAMPBELL ISLAND. ROCKHOPPER
PENGUINS BREED ON MANY SUBANTARCTIC ISLANDS AROUND
ANTARCTICA FROM THE FALKLANDS TO CROZET
AND MACQUARIE.

227 ELEPHANT SEALS (MIROUNGA LEONINA) BREED ON ALL
THE SUBANTARCTIC ISLANDS AROUND ANTARCTICA – HERE
THEY ARE ON CAMPBELL ISLAND. THEIR BREEDING SUCCESS,
HOWEVER, IS CLOSELY LINKED TO THE AVAILABILITY OF THEIR
FOOD SOURCES, WHICH CAN FLUCTUATE WITH EVEN MINOR
CHANGES TO THE SEA'S TEMPERATURE.

The New Zealand Subantarctic Islands

The Buller's albatross has soft, smoky-gray plumage, a bright yellow beak, and a fierce, proud stare, emphasized by the delicate markings around the eye. These noble creatures have a way about them that is both seductive and serene. To watch this graceful bird come in to land and occupy its pedestal-shaped nest after a prolonged buffeting over the Southern Ocean, is a reminder of just how precious these great fliers are. Ten albatross species call these islands home with no less than five of them, the southern royal, white-capped, antipodean, Campbell, and Gibson's wandering albatrosses, breeding nowhere else.

There are also some 20 species of petrels, fulmars, shearwaters, and prions that feed at sea all day then, at dusk, after circling overhead in great swirling flocks, dart in to land and occupy their burrows in the soft peaty soil or under tree roots. Like the albatrosses, these birds are all known as "tube nosed," due to the nostril-shaped canal on top of their beaks that helps to excrete salt from salt water, a crucial adaptation for birds that live most of their life at sea.

228 A BULLER'S ALBATROSS (THALASSRACHE BULLERI) INVESTIGATING POTENTIAL NEST SITES ON A CLIFF, MOLLYMAWK BAY, SNARES ISLANDS.

228-229 A BLACK-BROWED ALBATROSS (THALASSRACHE MELANOPHRIS) FEEDING ITS CHICK WITH SQUID, BULL ROCK, CAMPBELL ISLAND.

229 TOP A BLACK-BROWED ALBATROSS COLONY AT BULL ROCK, CAMPBELL ISLAND. ALBATROSSES COMMONLY NEST ON CLIFF TOPS SO THEY CAN UTILIZE THE WIND AND UPDRAFTS TO GET AIRBORNE. ONCE AIRBORNE, AN ALBATROSS CAN GLIDE FOR MANY WEEKS, RIDING EVEN THE SLIGHTEST AIR CURRENTS ON ITS LONG FLIGHT OVER THE SOUTHERN OCEAN IN SEARCH OF SQUID.

Four penguin species also come and go from their nests that are tucked away in the tangle of *Hebe* scrub and contorted *Olearia*, a tree daisy. Two penguin species, the Snares crested and the erect crested, are endemic. Overall, New Zealand is home to six penguin species, which is the greatest diversity of penguin species in the world. There are also three endemic shag subspecies, as well as 15 specialized ground birds, such as the Campbell island snipe, which was only discovered in 1997, and the flightless Campbell island teal.

The subantarctic islands in general have a harsh climate, however, the cluster of islands that make up the Snares group is the most temperate of all, with an average temperature of 52°F (11°C) and an annual rainfall of 47 inches (1,200 mm). Unlike the other islands, snow is uncommon on the Snares, and they have the distinction of being the only forested group that has never been contaminated by introduced mammals. There are 20 species of higher plants on the Snares that are completely indigenous (including rare megaherbs), plus many unusual mosses, lichens, and fungi. After emerging from the *Olearia* trees with their wind-twisted branches, the funny little Snares crested penguins launch themselves off the granite cliffs and swim out to sea through long swirling bands of kelp. At dusk it is an amazing spectacle to witness the flocks of sooty shearwaters circling overhead, then to see them crash in through the forest canopy to scurry away into their burrows. Much of the forest's leaf litter has been dragged inside to create cosy underground nests. On the Snares alone there are thought to be six million shearwaters.

230-231 SNARES CRESTED PENGUINS (EUDYPTES ROBUTUS) ON A ROCK PLATFORM WITH BULL KELP SURGING IN THE SURF, SNARES ISLAND. KELP, KNOWN AS THE FASTEST GROWING PLANT IN THE WORLD, GROWS IN LONG FEATHERY STRANDS AROUND ALL SUBANTARCTIC ISLANDS, MAKING IT HARD FOR PENGUINS OR SEALS TO SWIM THEIR WAY TO SHORE THROUGH THIS SUBMARINE FOREST.

The Auckland Islands are the largest and highest (Mt. Raynal is the highest peak at 2,112 ft/644 m) of the five groups, with the main island some 25 miles (40 km) long, consisting of two ancient volcanoes that are now largely covered in tussock grass. Smaller offshore islands, such as Disapointment, Adams, and Enderby, are truly special places for wildlife, both as breeding grounds for albatrosses on the steep vegetated cliffs on Adams and Disappointment, and, in the case of Enderby, home for a breeding colony of the rare and endemic Hooker's (now called New Zealand) sea lions (total population 12,000). On a good day, the clear turquoise waters and grass-lined beach of Enderby's Sandy Bay appear so idyllic that it is hard to believe this is a subantarctic island and not a Polynesian one.

To complete this tropical illusion, a cheeky red-crowned parakeet flits out of a red-flowering rata tree behind the beach to land at your feet. Then a quartet of shy, yellow-eyed penguins parade past, waddling across the yellow sand to disappear furtively into the forest. South of Enderby, in the main island's Port Ross, pods of the once-hunted southern right whales gather during winter months to enjoy the shelter of the bay and give birth to their calves and to mate. Some eight million years ago volcanic activity played a major role in the formation of Campbell Island. The island's highest peak is Mt. Honey (1,866 ft/569 m) situated above a major fjord-like inlet, Perseverance Harbour. Campbell hosts more species of albatross (six) than any other subantarctic island except Crozet, the French island in the Southern Indian Ocean which has seven. The Campbell mollymawk (the smaller albatross species are known collectively as mollymawks) is endemic here, though the island is justly famous as a major breeding ground for the southern royal albatross, which nests on the higher, open tussock grass slopes. This is the main stronghold for the world's rarest and most endangered penguin, the yellow-eyed penguin, and there are some 600 breeding pairs.

232 FALLEN RATA FLOWERS LITTER THE FOREST FLOOR, ENDERBY ISLAND, IN THE AUCKLAND ISLANDS GROUP.

232-233 FLOWERING RATA FOREST, ENDERBY ISLAND, WITH AUCKLAND ISLAND IN THE DISTANCE.

234-235 A WATERFALL DROPPING FROM A HANGING VALLEY
INTO A RATA FOREST, MCLENNAN INLET, AUCKLAND ISLAND. THE
AUCKLAND ISLANDS HAVE AN ESPECIALLY RUGGED LANDSCAPE
WITH STEEP-SIDED CLIFFS AND AN ALMOST IMPENETRABLE
FOREST OF NATIVE TREES, SUCH AS THE RED-FLOWERING RATA.

235 RED-CROWNED PARAKEETS (CYANORAMPHUS
NOVAEZELANDIAE) LIVE IN THE RATA FOREST, ENDERBY
ISLAND. THE RED-CROWNED PARAKEET IS COMMON TO AT
LEAST FIVE ISLANDS WITHIN THE AUCKLAND ISLANDS. THERE IS
ALSO A YELLOW-CROWNED PARAKEET.

The New Zealand
Subantarctic Islands

236 NEW ZEALAND (HOOKER'S) SEA LION COW (PHOCARCTOS
HOOKERI) WITH A SUCKLING PUP, ENDERBY ISLAND.

236-237 A NEW ZEALAND (HOOKER'S) SEA LION COW
(PHOCARCTOS HOOKERI) SPARRING WITH A YOUNG BULL
AT PERSEVERANCE HARBOUR, CAMPBELL ISLAND.

237 TOP NEW ZEALAND (HOOKER'S) SEA LION PUPS PLAY IN A CRÈCHE, ENDERBY ISLAND. NEW ZEALAND (HOOKER'S) SEA LIONS ARE ENDEMIC TO NEW ZEALAND'S SUBANTARCTIC ISLANDS, BUT HAVE BECOME ENDANGERED IN RECENT YEARS DUE TO THE PUPS DYING IN COLLAPSED RABBIT BURROWS (THE RABBITS HAVE BEEN ERADICATED) OR DROWNED AS A BY-CATCH IN FISHING NETS.

238-239 A DIVER HAS A CLOSE ENCOUNTER WITH A
SOUTHERN RIGHT WHALE (EUBALAENA AUSTRALIS). THE
SOUTHERN RIGHT WHALE HAS A CIRCUMPOLAR POPULATION
DISTRIBUTED THROUGHOUT THE SOUTHERN OCEAN, WHICH
MOVES FURTHER SOUTH TO THE COLDER ANTARCTIC WATERS
TO FEED DURING THE SUMMER MONTHS. THESE WHALES ARE
KNOWN TO BE CURIOUS TO AND INTERACT WITH OTHER SEA
CREATURES SUCH AS SEALS.

Antarctica

The New Zealand Subantarctic Islands

240 AN ERECT-CRESTED PENGUIN (EUDYPTES SCLATERI)
GUARDS ITS CHICK, ANTIPODES ISLAND.

240-241 A PAIR OF ERECT-CRESTED PENGUINS ON A NEST
OVERLOOKING THE ORDE-LEES COLONY ON THE NORTH
COAST OF ANTIPODES ISLAND.

To the east of the main island groups lie the remote and rarely visited Bounty and Antipodes islands – tiny specs of rainswept granite amid the vast Southern Ocean. The next subantarctic island group to the east is the South Shetland Islands near the Antarctic Peninsula, at least 4,970 miles (8,000 km) away across the southern reaches of the Pacific Ocean. The Bounty Islands are named for H.M.S. *Bounty* which sailed past here in 1788 under the command of Captain William Bligh. While the treeless Antipodes are tussock covered, the Bounties are almost devoid of vegetation. Bligh thought them snow-covered, however, it was almost certainly seabird guano that caught his attention.

The Antipodes and Bounties, just like their bigger neighbors Campbell and the Aucklands, receive a continual pounding from the prevailing westerly winds. Again, seabirds are the highlight and focus for the sporadic visits by scientists, conservationists, and tourists who all have to make difficult landings from a ship. The antipodean wandering albatross is the principal attraction, as it is considered a separate species to the Gibson's wandering from Campbell Island. Two little penguins, raucous in the extreme, and seemingly constantly fighting, the erect-crested and rockhoppers also breed on the Antipodes in great numbers. The Antipodes even has its very own parakeet, *Cyanoramphus unicolor*, with distinctive emerald green plumage and is a larger bird than the red-crowned parakeet, which also lives on the Antipodes. In a curious coexistence perhaps brought about by a shortage of suitable nesting sites, the penguins of the Bounty Islands nest freely among the albatrosses. Along the rocky coastlines some 20,000 New Zealand fur seals also breed here. As occurred on most of the subantarctic islands, these fur seals were slaughtered in great numbers during the 19th century for their valuable pelts. Thankfully now, their populations have recovered.

It is a great comfort to know that beyond the Roaring Forties a network of subantarctic islands exist where the species have been so little impacted by human activity. These wonderful island sanctuaries are home to birds and animals that no longer fear the presence of humans, where they will continue to happily approach a person with an innate curiosity. Long may this trust remain.

The New Zealand Subantarctic Islands

244-245 SALVIN'S ALBATROSSES (THALASSARCHE SALVINI)
RETURN EN MASSE TO THE CROWDED NESTING COLONY AT
DUSK ON PROCLAMATION ISLAND, BOUNTY ISLANDS.

245 A SALVIN'S ALBATROSS LANDING AT SUNSET AT THE
BREEDING COLONY ON PROCLAMATION ISLAND IN THE BOUNTY
ISLANDS. THESE BEAUTIFUL OCEAN-GOING SEABIRDS ALSO
BREED ON CROZET AND SNARES ISLANDS, AS WELL AS OTHER
ISLANDS IN THE BOUNTY GROUP. THEY BUILD SMALL PEDESTAL
NESTS MADE FROM MUD, GUANO, OR SMALL ROCK CHIPS.

Macquarie Island

Hidden away at 54 degrees South, the subantarctic Macquarie Island is another tiny speck of land that is seemingly cast adrift on the vast Southern Ocean. Cold, wet, and battered by the incessant westerly winds of the Furious Fifties, Macquarie lies 920 miles (1,480 km) southeast of Tasmania. The island is designated a nature reserve and is now administered by the Tasmanian Parks and Wildlife Service, though much of its scientific program is controlled by the Hobart-based Australian Antarctic Division. A marine reserve has also been established right round the island to protect the rich diversity of marine life that is attracted to Macquarie to breed. In 1977, UNESCO declared the island a Biosphere Reserve as part of its Biosphere Program. Twenty years later, in 1997, Macquarie was designated a UNESCO World Heritage Site.

In addition to Macquarie's intrinsic beauty, the island is of immense interest to scientists. For geologists it provides a unique example of seafloor strata raised above sea level to become dry land in a mid-ocean location. Macquarie was forced up from the seafloor about 700,000 years ago by the collision of the Australian and Pacific tectonic plates. The island has never been attached to any other landmass. Its closest neighbour is the New Zealand subantarctic Campbell Island. It is largely due to this geological uniqueness that Macquarie was given World Heritage status.

Biologists, too, come to Macquarie to make use of the year-round base that clings to a thin strip of land at the extreme north end of the island. During the frequent storms that lash the island, big waves wash over this narrow sandy gap between Hasselborough and Buckles' bays, but antipodean biologists are tough and they are happy to withstand the salt spray, wind, and mud in order to study the multitude of seabirds, penguins, seals, and plants that call Macquarie home. The plants and animals are of interest both as survivors of long-distance dispersal and for being able to tolerate Macquarie's severe subantarctic climate. The island lies roughly 170 miles (270 km) north of Antarctica's biological boundary, the Antarctic Convergence Zone, where cold and warm ocean currents mix. Macquarie, therefore, is surrounded by food-rich seas that sustain the island's many seabirds and sea mammals.

For meteorologists, climatologists, and physicists, Macquarie provides one of the few land-based stations for monitoring southern, high latitude climatic and atmospheric phenomena. The island is of particular interest to ionospheric physicists because it is at the right latitude to observe spectacular displays of Aurora Australis.

246 THOUSANDS OF ROYAL PENGUINS (EUDYPTES SCHLEGELI) ON THEIR NESTING SITES, LAYING EGGS AND REARING THEIR CHICKS, SANDY BAY.

246-247 WHILE A GROUP OF PENGUINS LOOK ON, ELEPHANT SEALS SNOOZE ON A BEACH ON THE NORTH COAST DURING THE SUMMER MOULTING SEASON.

247 TOP THE MASSIVE KING PENGUIN (APTENODYTES PATAGONICUS) COLONY AT LUSITANIA BAY, MACQUARIE ISLAND, IS ONE OF THE GREAT WILDLIFE SPECTACLES. THE TUSSOCK-COVERED HILLS BEHIND THE COLONY GIVE A GOOD IMPRESSION OF THE RUGGED LANDSCAPE OF THIS BEAUTIFUL AUSTRALIAN SUBANTARCTIC ISLAND.

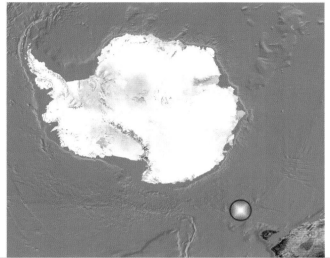

Macquarie Island

Although Macquarie now enjoys total protection, this was not always the case. As early as 1810, Macquarie Island was first put on the map by a Sydney-based sealing vessel. Some of the crew were landed on the shingle beaches so they could begin the grizzly work of massacring the fur and elephant seals for their pelts and oil-rich blubber, which was much needed in those days as a source of lighting oil, lubricants, and for use in paint. Over 20,000 fur seals were taken in the first 18 months. This slaughter continued for the best part of 100 years, though the fur seals were almost exterminated in a decade. Eventually, at Luisitania Bay on the southeast coast, even the macaroni and king penguins were marched up planks of wood to die a horrible death in boiling cauldrons called digesters, where up to 2,000 at a time were rendered down into oil. Unlike islands such as South Georgia, Macquarie was never a base for whaling operations, in part due to the difficulty of landing and the lack of a safe harbor.

The famous Australian Antarctic geologist and explorer Douglas Mawson helped to bring this brutal industry to an end. Mawson's Australasian Antarctic expedition of 1911–14 erected radio masts and established a wireless relay station on Macquarie as the island was roughly half way between the Australian mainland and the Antarctic continent. By 1915, with the oil industry run by New Zealanders and the island almost under New Zealand control, Mawson began actively campaigning to have Macquarie fully protected. Lobbying continued until 1933 before Macquarie was formally designated as an Australian wildlife sanctuary. Unfortunately, the early human occupation had an impact on the native species as foreign plants, black rats, mice, wekas (a New Zealand ground hen), cats, and, sadly, rabbits were left behind after the oil industry declined. The introduction of alien animal species led directly to the extinction of two endemic birds; a flightless rail and a parakeet. Today, despite many attempts to eradicate them with guns and the virus myxoma, the rabbits have prospered, causing significant damage to vast swathes of tussock grass. The lack of an effective rabbit eradication programme on Macquarie is a national disgrace and needs urgent attention.

Macquarie island is an elongated rectangle 21 miles (34 km) long by 3 miles (5 km) wide, consisting of an undulating plateau covered with tussock grass about 650 ft (200 m) above sea level. At 1,453 ft (443 m), Mt. Hamilton is the highest point. The treeless almost barren feldmark, tundra-like ground on the plateau is dotted with lakes and streams, and it drops off steeply to narrow shingle beaches and wild surf. The island is famous for the Macquarie Island cabbage (*Stilbocarpa polaris*), which provided a valuable source of vitamin C for sailors and so help ward off scurvy. Although snow can fall at any time at these latitudes there are no permanent snowfields or glaciers on the island, and there is never any sea ice. Wind, temperature, cloud cover, and precipitation vary very little throughout the year, though day length shortens dramatically during the winter months. Earthquakes are reasonably common on the sub-surface Macquarie Ridge and the island itself sits astride a major fault system that runs northwards into the South Island of New Zealand, known there as the Alpine fault.

248 PYRAMID LAKE ON THE HIGHLAND PLATEAU OF MACQUARIE ISLAND IS SURROUNDED BY LUSH ALPINE VEGETATION.

248-249 TYPICAL HIGHLAND PLATEAU VEGETATION WITH CUSHIONS OF AZORELLA MACQUARIENSIS AND MT. WAITE IN THE DISTANCE.

249 TOP SAWYER'S CREEK WATERFALL TUMBLES DOWN FROM MACQUARIE ISLAND'S HIGHLAND PLATEAU AS IT FLOWS TOWARDS THE SEA.

It is the island's seabirds that are justly famous and attract many visitors each year who brave the rigorous ocean passage from Hobart. To see the macaroni and king penguin beaches of Macquarie is one of the great wildlife spectacles on this planet. The largest macaroni penguin colony in the world, with half a million pairs, is located at Hurd Point on the southern tip of the island. Lusitania Bay is a truly stunning place for wildlife as well, hosting some 200,000 breeding pairs of glistening king penguins with their beautiful black and orange heads and distinctive trumpeting call. Gentoos and rockhopper penguins also breed on Macquarie. Among the 72 species of birds recorded on the island there are four species of albatross, the light-mantled sooty albatross, the wandering albatross, the black-browed albatross, and the grey-headed albatross. Sadly, all species are struggling to maintain their numbers because of predators such as feral cats and also because they are being killed as a bycatch of the fishing industry.

Sharing the beaches with the penguins are large numbers of elephant seals and three species of fur seals, principally the New Zealand fur seal (*Arctocephalus forsteri*). The southern elephant seal (*Mirounga leonina*) reached a population peak of 110,000 in the 1950s, but numbers have since declined. Although the submarine shelf around Macquarie is narrow, it is still rich in marine life. The giant bull kelp (*Durvillaea antarctica*) provides a highly productive habitat for plankton and fish, which in turn support the seals and birds.

Although Australia administers two major subantarctic islands, McDonald Island and the glaciated and actively volcanic Heard Island, Macquarie Island is undoubtedly the jewel in the Aussie crown. Along with the nearby New Zealand subantarctic islands, both groups of islands form important sanctuaries for the wildlife of the Southern Ocean.

250-251 EXPOSED TO THE SOUTHERN OCEAN WIND, WITH LITTLE MORE THAN TUSSOCK GRASS FOR SHELTER, A COLONY OF ROYAL PENGUINS (EUDYPTES SCHLEGELI) WILL LAY THEIR EGGS AND RAISE CHICKS DURING THE SUMMER.

252 *A PAIR OF ROCKHOPPER PENGUINS (EUDYPTES CHRYSOCOME) SHELTERING UNDER MACQUARIE ISLAND CABBAGE.*

252-253 *ROYAL PENGUINS (EUDYPTES SCHLEGELI) MOVING THROUGH MEGAHERBS TOWARDS THE SEA, FINCH CREEK, MACQUARIE ISLAND.*

254-255 *A PAIR OF ROYAL PENGUINS (EUDYPTES SCHLEGELI) SNOOZE IN THE SUMMER SUN ON A TYPICAL ROCKY BEACH, MACQUARIE ISLAND.*

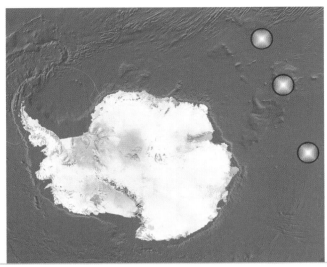

256 TOP THE RUGGED COASTLINE OF
COURBET PENINSULA IN THE
KERGUELEN ARCHIPELAGO.

256-257 A CROWDED KING PENGUIN
(APTENODYTES PATAGONICUS)
COLONY ON CROZET ISLAND.
THE JOSTLING CROWD INCLUDES
BOTH ADULTS AND BROWN,
DOWN-COVERED CHICKS.

ANTARCTICA - ANTARCTICA - ANTARCTICA - ANTARCTIC

The Subantarctic Islands of the Southern Indian Ocean

The southern Indian Ocean contains a stunning array of rugged subantarctic island nature reserves that are administered by South Africa, France, and Australia. Although each one is well north of 60 degrees South and so beyond the protection of the Antarctic Treaty, any visitor stepping ashore must have prior permission and is legally obliged to abide by the strictest possible environmental code. The distance between each of these remote wildlife sanctuaries is truly daunting, especially as everyone must undertake an arduous sea voyage to get to them across the Southern Ocean, effectively taking on the might of the Roaring Forties and the Furious Fifties. As such, these beautiful islands are rarely visited and are usually the preserve of scientists undertaking approved university or government scientific research. Their very isolation is their best protection.

Some 1,840 miles (2,960 km) east of Norway's Bouvetoya Island lies South Africa's Marion and Prince Edward islands. These two bleak island groups are roughly southeast from the Cape of Good Hope. Further east, for another storm-tossed 575 miles (925 km), lies France's Iles Crozet, and then it is another 860 miles (1,380 km) eastward to France's Iles Kerguelen. Northeast from Kerguelen lies the even more remote St. Paul and Amsterdam islands. Then comes Australia's Heard and McDonald island group, located only 310 miles (500 km) to the southeast of Kerguelen. From Heard, it is a huge 3,680 miles (5,900 km) eastward to the next subantarctic island, Australia's Macquarie Island.

The southern Indian Ocean is not a place for the fainthearted mariner. Typically, these latitudes are a stormy and dangerous environment that feature incessant gales, constant hail, snow and pelting rain then, almost unbelievably, utter calm and mist … and just when you let your guard down, the heavy subantarctic swell takes charge again … pure bliss for the wildlife and wilderness enthusiast.

These islands are all volcanic in origin, though Heard Island's Big Ben massif is the only persistently active volcano among them. Kerguelen, however, does have glaciers and permanent snowfields, and its highest peak at 6,069 ft (1,850 m) is the volcano Pic du Grand-Ross. There are still active volcanic fumeroles in the southwest of the main island, Grande Terre. Being right on the Antarctic Convergence Zone at 49 degrees South, there is never any sea ice around Kerguelen. Occasional icebergs, however, do drift this far north.

Iles Kerguelen (initially known as Desolation Island) was discovered as early as 1772 by the French navigator Captain Yves-Joseph de Kerguelen-Tremarec. Captain James Cook, in 1776, also helped to put Kerguelen firmly on the rapidly evolving map of new-found land in the southern latitudes. As happened on almost every subantarctic island around the rim of the Southern Ocean, it wasn't long before whalers and sealers came to hunt the whales, elephant seals, and fur seals. The island also became famous with early mariners for the Kerguelen cabbage (*Pringlea antiscorbutica*), which, as the name suggests, provided an important source of vitamin C in an otherwise unhealthy seaman's diet.

Kerguelen is a large island (74 miles/120 km by 68 miles/110 km), however, because there are so many deep fjords, no part of the island is more than 12 miles (20 km) from the sea. Kerguelen has a large permanent French research station at Port aux France (up to 110 staff in summer, 70 in winter), which is part of the government's Terres Australes et Antarctiques Francaises. The main island itself has, sadly, over the years, been heavily impacted by invasive foreign species. Grande Terre has sheep (the now rare Bizet sheep), Corsican mountain sheep, rabbits, reindeer, cattle, cats, rats, and even salmon. Mink were taken there, too, with a few swimming to some of the 300 smaller outlying islands. Thankfully, Kerguelen still has healthy populations of king, gentoo, macaroni, and rockhopper penguins. Albatrosses use Kerguelen's wild coastline as a breeding ground and launch pad for their feeding forays into the Southern Ocean. The island is home to the mighty wandering, black-browed, gray-headed, and light-mantled sooty albatrosses as well as a host of petrels and prion species.

The Subantarctic Islands
of the Southern Indian Ocean

Known collectively as the Prince Edward Islands, Marion and Prince Edward islands have been politically part of South Africa since 1947. They are located at 46 degrees South, some 1,150 miles (1,850 km) southeast of Port Elizabeth in South Africa. Marion, the larger of the two volcanic islands, has a small research base whose staff conduct meteorological and biological work. The highest summit is the 4,074 ft (1,242 m) high Mascarin Peak. It is commonly cloud-covered as the islands attract foul weather with heavy rain and strong winds on at least 320 days each year. Mascarin last erupted in 1980 and so it is classified as an active volcano.

Although first sighted in 1663, Marion Island was only approached again in 1772 by Marc-Joseph Marion du Fresne who spent five days trying to land, thinking he had discovered the long-postulated great southern landmass of Terre Australis Incognita – Antarctica. It was the ubiquitous Captain James Cook who later named the other island Prince Edward Island, though he, too, failed to make a landing.

In 1949, five cats were introduced to deal with a long-standing mice problem, but the cats multiplied rapidly and the population exploded to over 3,400 by 1977. Naturally, the cats had a devastating impact on the burrowing petrels and other seabirds and had to be hunted to reduce their numbers. It is now thought that all the cats have been exterminated. Five million penguins breed on the Prince Edward Islands. Some two million of them are the spectacularly graceful king penguin, who live in five main colonies. There are colonies of gentoos, rockhoppers, and macaronis. Royal penguins have also been observed as casual visitors, however, they do not breed on the islands. Five albatross species breed here, with the approximately 3,000 pairs of wandering albatrosses comprising the biggest population.

Some 2,400 miles (3,860 km) southwest of Perth, Western Australia, lie Heard and McDonald islands. These were the last of the subantarctic islands of the Southern Indian Ocean to be discovered, with the first sighting in 1833. Successful landings were eventually made in 1854

and then in 1874 by the crew from the Challenger Scientific Expedition. Both islands are volcanic with Heard's heavily glaciated Big Ben massif being particularly active. At 9,005 ft (2,745 m) Mawson Peak is the highest peak in the massif and is Australia's highest summit. Some 15 major glaciers flow down from Big Ben, often ending as high ice cliffs on the coast. These barriers make progress around the island on foot very difficult. The ice-free McDonald Island, only 26 miles (42 km) west of Heard, had been dormant for 75,000 years, but several eruptions have occurred over the past few years, with the most recent in 2005.

Heard and McDonald islands have been part of Australian territory since 1947 and the group was declared a World Heritage Site in 1997. Heard Island was named for an American sealer who sighted the islands in 1853. This inevitably resulted in the bloody plunder of the fur seal population, which lasted until 1880 by which time the animals were nearly exterminated. During this period, up to 200 sealers lived onshore in dank huts. Australia administered a scientific base at Atlas Cove from 1947 to 1955 and the island became a totally protected reserve. The sealers' huts were finally removed in 2001.

At 53 degrees South, Heard is just on the polar side of the Antarctic Convergence Zone. It therefore does not get sea ice during the winter. Leopard seals are frequent visitors, though fur and elephant seals are the main pinniped (fin-footed) species to be found on the beaches. Heard is home to over two million macaroni penguins and 100,000 breeding pairs of king penguins raise their brown barrel-shaped chicks there. Fortunately, foreign species have never been introduced to this stunning wild island.

It is to be hoped that France and South Africa will continue to eliminate introduced plant and animal species from all the islands under their control. This is an urgent priority, too, at Australia's Macquarie Island. Each of these subantarctic islands of the South Indian Ocean are precious sanctuaries for seabirds and sea mammals, warranting the highest degree of environmental protection possible.

Vanishing Wilderness of **Antarctica**

The Subantarctic Islands of the Southern Indian Ocean

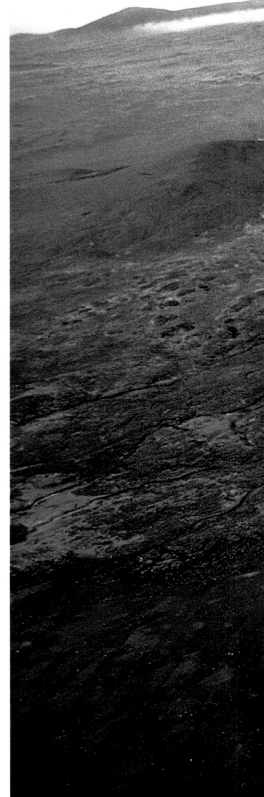

Also under French control, Iles Crozet is another island group of six, main volcanic islands situated at 46 degrees South. Since 1963, France has maintained a 30-person research station called Alfred Faure and conducts biological, geological, and meteorological work on a year-round basis. Crozet was discovered by the French explorer Marc-Joseph Marion du Fresne who landed on Ile de la Possession in 1772, naming the Crozet group after his second-in-command. Crozet is renowned for its rain and wind. Despite the dismal weather there is a massive population of macaroni penguins of two million pairs who take up residence during the summer breeding season. Gentoo and rockhopper penguins have also established colonies on Crozet. There is also a major population of king penguins, perhaps the largest colony in the world. Orca regularly patrol the beaches in search of seal pups or unwary penguins and are known to launch themselves up onto the beaches in their final lunge for a meal, which is a difficult maneuver that requires great skill to wriggle back into the sea with the next surge of surf. This method of attack has also been observed on Argentina's Patagonian coast.

Crozet has been a nature reserve since 1938, though it was originally administered as a dependency of Madagascar. The once pristine ecosystem has been damaged by the introduction of cats and rats. At least the introduced goats and pigs have now been exterminated. They were taken to Crozet for food for the many shipwrecked castaways who ended up on the island. In 1887, the French ship *Tamaris* was wrecked and stranded on the Ile des Cochons. The crew tied a note to the leg of a wandering albatross which was recovered seven months later in Western Australia.

260 A MALE ELEPHANT SEAL (MIROUNGA LEONINA) WITH HIS HAREM LIES ON A WINDSWEPT BEACH ON MARION ISLAND.

260-261 AN AERIAL VIEW OF ILE DE L'EST IN THE CROZET ARCHIPELAGO.

261 TOP A MOULTING ROCKHOPPER PENGUIN (EUDYPTES CHRYSOCOME) WAITS FOR HIS NEW PLUMAGE TO COME THROUGH BEFORE HE CAN GO BACK TO FEED AT SEA, CROZET ISLANDS.

The Subantarctic Islands of the Southern Indian Ocean

262-263 A LIGHT-MANTLED SOOTY ALBATROSS (PHOEBETRIA PALPEBRATA) HAS FOUND A SHELTERED LEDGE FOR ITS NEST, CROZET ISLANDS.

263 A LIGHT-MANTLED SOOTY ALBATROSS FLIES ACROSS A TUSSOCK-COVERED HEADLAND, CROZET ISLANDS.

The Subantarctic Islands
of the Southern Indian Ocean

264 TOP AN ELEGANT CAMPBELL BLACK-BROWED ALBATROSS
(DIOMEDEA MELANOPHRYS IMPAVIDA) IS LANDING
AT ITS NESTING PLACE IN THE BULL ROCK COLONY,
CAMPBELL ISLAND.

264 BOTTOM A SPERM WHALE (PHYSETER MACROCEPHALUS)
DIVES OFF THE COAST OF THE CROZET ISLANDS IN SEARCH

OF SQUID, WHICH IS ITS MAIN FOOD SOURCE.
THEY CAN DIVE TO INCREDIBLE DEPTHS AND HOLD THEIR
BREATH FOR OVER HALF AN HOUR.

264-265 THE PROMONTORIES TO THE WEST OF THE SNARES
ISLANDS WERE SO CALLED BECAUSE IT WAS CONSIDERED
DANGEROUS TO ATTEMPT AN APPROACH TO THE COAST.

266 A MASSIVE ELEPHANT SEAL (MIROUNGA LEONINA)
DWARFS A CURIOUS KING PENGUIN (APTENODYTES
PATAGONICUS), CROZET ISLANDS.

266-267 A MALE ELEPHANT SEAL LOOKS OUT TO SEA FROM
THE MIDDLE OF A KING PENGUIN (APTENODYTES
PATAGONICUS) COLONY, CROZET ISLANDS.

PHOTO CREDITS - PHOTO CREDITS - PHOTO CREDITS - PH

272 A COUPLE OF EMPEROR PENGUINS
(APTENODYTES FORSTERI) DURING COURTSHIP.

WHITE STAR PUBLISHERS

WS White Star Publishers® is a registered trademark
property of Edizioni White Star s.r.l.

© 2010 Edizioni White Star s.r.l.
Via Candido Sassone, 24
13100 Vercelli, Italy
www.whitestar.it

Editing: Sam Merrell

ISBN 978-88-544-0487-8
1 2 3 4 5 6   14 13 12 11 10

Printed in Indonesia